Life Stories

Unworthy Servant

Ken Scott
(1949–)

2020

© 2020 Lulu Author: Ken Scott.
All rights reserved.
ISBN 978-0-244-55634-1

Contents

Foreword			5
Introduction			7
1	Bible College and Pre-Peru	1968-1973	10
2	Costa Rica	1973-1974	13
3	Abancay, Apurimac	1974	17
4	Our Wedding	1974	21
5	Chalhuanca	1975-1978	23
6	First Furlough	1978-1979	32
7	Andahuaylas, Apurimac	1979-1980	35
8	Second Furlough	1980-1981	37
9	Abancay, Apurimac	1981-1984	39
10	Third Furlough	1984-1985	47
11	Lima	1985-1987	49
12	Fourth Furlough	1987-1988	52
13	Lima	1989-1991	54
14	Belfast Bible College	1991-1999	58
15	Baptist Missions	2000-2007	63
16	Irish Baptist College	2008-2014	71
17	Retirement	2014-	74
18	Reflections		80
Appendix A	When the Earth trembles		84
Appendix B	Health & Wealth		86
Appendix C	Humility is a Pilgrimage		91
Appendix D	Thoughts on Leadership		94

Acknowledgements

I have turned my mind to writing this page while the process of editing the manuscript of the book is in the able hands of Graham and Heather Lyttle. I have already witnessed their expertise and improvements to the text, especially in the realm of punctuation. I have never finally learned how to employ commas! It is difficult to include a list of all those to whom I owe a debt of gratitude and I freely accept that the words that follow will be inadequate and incomplete.

I am indebted to the Lyttles, mentioned above, and to John Robinson, an elder in Newtownbreda Baptist Church, for reading the manuscript and for their encouragement and advice. My oldest brother Tom and his wife Elizabeth have been their usual magnanimous selves by reading the first draft and by making helpful suggestions. I owe similar comments with regard to my sister Doreen and her husband Gordon. Our son Samuel is currently reading our draft-book and his observations will enrich the finished product as they come in.

The final title to be employed became a matter for discussion and all those mentioned above made contributions. Jeannie and I mutually agreed that the best choice for this story would be *Life Stories of an* **Unworthy** *Servant.* The competing adjective was **Unprofitable.** This leads me in my thinking to remember to thank God for His mercy (in not giving me what I deserved), for His grace (in showering on me through Christ what I have not deserved) and for giving me the privilege of seeking to hear Him through the Scriptures and by the Holy Spirit, to see Him with the eyes of faith and to follow Him, albeit very falteringly. I reflect with gratitude to the Lord.

Many people deserve a mention here and I trust that the book will illustrate who some of them are. My parents, siblings, relatives and upbringing in the Orkney Isles hold a place in my heart and formed me into who I am. Of course, my wife Jeannie, since I met her in 1973, is the person who has enriched my life the most. Together, Jeannie and I have had the joy of serving God near and far and of bringing up two children, Rebecca and Samuel. Rebecca, along with her husband Ganesh, brought two grandchildren into our lives—Anjali and Ajay—who introduced us to a new and rich stage of life.

The "stories" that follow are only a select few of some of those that could be included. There are others that are still too emotionally challenging to be told by me. Finally, I acknowledge full responsibility for the content of this book and for its limitations.

Foreword

I remember reading the autobiography (760 pages) of one of the great Christian evangelists of my lifetime. I quickly decided that I would have to tackle the book slowly as I plodded through what seemed to me to be a day-in-the-life of the evangelist as I read similar reports of one international evangelistic campaign after another. Nevertheless, I felt rewarded when I came across reflective moments when "gems" in the book made it all worth the effort.

This book does not pretend to imitate the above-mentioned tome nor to compare myself to the great evangelist mentioned in the previous paragraph, but I do dare to suggest that I am not unlike many others who follow Christ. I will attempt to be selective, brief and will cut to the chase. What follows is as eclectic as our lives and the furnishings in our home. As both Jeannie and I reached our seventieth birthdays in January 2019 we look back and marvel as to how quickly we have arrived here! We are not old, although we may appear "retro" to some!

We are both quite ordinary and do not claim any other status. Jeannie, born to Mennonite parents in Greenwood Delaware, was the tenth child in a family of thirteen surviving siblings (nine sisters and four brothers)—there were 13, now 11 remain. I was born to Baptist parents in the Orkney Islands, the fourth son of a total of eight siblings (seven brothers and one sister!), all still alive at the time of writing.

Having just completed writing a rather academic book in Spanish[1], and having just returned from Peru, I decided to write briefly and to choose some illustrative life stories that have shaped my life. Some will be recounted while others will be redacted in the appendices from published articles in missionary magazines. Either way, they are backed up by life stories. I cannot write about myself without including Jeannie. More importantly, I cannot write about myself, and trust me, I have never liked focussing on myself, without highlighting the Lord Jesus Christ.

I remember very clearly that I gave all I knew of me to all I knew of Christ when ten years of age. I knew then that I was a sinner and that I needed Christ to be my Saviour. I now know more clearly that I am capable of more sin and that Christ is more glorious than I had realised then. It was clear to me then that, but for God's mercy and grace, I would not and could not know God. I have carried these truths with me and into my ongoing relationship with Christ from childhood and through all the phases of life.

Just before I move on, I want to make three comments. Firstly, on my chosen title for the book, Jeannie first drew my attention to something she had not

---

[1] Kenneth D. Scott Eunson, 2019, *Nuevos Movimientos Religiosos Andinos. Influencia del pentecostalismo en el pensamiento de Ezequiel Ataucusi*, Tomo II, Ediciones Puma.

"seen" before and that I have to confess, led me to "see" servanthood in a new light. After Jesus' teaching on the need for us to forgive in order to be forgiven (Luke 17:1–4), Luke records that the apostles said to the Lord, "Show us how to increase our faith" (v. 5). The surprise for me is in the reply that Jesus gave to their plea. After telling them what could be done through faith (v. 6), Jesus illustrated the need to be a faithful and dutiful servant (vs. 8–9) and then applies the illustration with these words: "So likewise you, when you have done all those things which you are commanded, say 'We are unprofitable servants. We have done what was our duty to do.'" (v. 10). Jesus said that.

Secondly, with sermonising over, and with a move to tales of this "unprofitable", "unworthy", "worthless" servant, I have sought to live my life in the light of God's mercy and grace and "by faith". I see life as a sequence of events controlled by God's providential hand at work in the events of the lives of His children. This is my story and it is not for me to relate that of anybody else. Furthermore, I will be as truthful as I can be without embellishment. What follows are memories indelibly etched on my mind and heart. I trust you will read on and allow me to tell you a few of the stories of an aging servant.

Thirdly, and following on from my second comment, I have had some years to reflect on an often-quoted Bible verse. Romans 8:28 states: "And we know that in all things God works for the good of those who love him, who have been called according to his purpose". We misread the Bible when we assume that "we" automatically means "me". The verse was sent by Paul, in the first instance, to Christians in Rome facing persecution. This verse should not be used to reflect retrospectively in order to explain that everything will become clear with hindsight. Paul did not promise the Christians in Rome that all the things that happened, and were about to happen ("trouble or hardship or persecution or famine or nakedness or danger or sword" 8:35), were good. Everything that happens is not good. This verse is not a promise that God will protect us from all harm and heartache. Therefore, not all that happens is the will of God. Nevertheless God, in His providence would then, and now, bring about His purposes, and that is good.

Introduction

> "Day by day nothing seems to change
> but when you look back everything is different.
> And it is."
> C. S. Lewis

Orkney may well have had its Christian times in history, but I believe it is fair to suggest that I was aware of very few other professing Christians as I grew up. This was especially clear to me at school where such views were ridiculed by classmates and sometimes by teachers. This only made me stronger. There were the Baptists, the Brethren, the Catholics and some Presbyterians. My father taught me his theology of separation of Church and State and, by example, that wherever we meet another Christian—a sinner saved by the grace of God—we should have fellowship. We were few and far between in Orkney at that time. Things have moved on since, especially with the introduction of evangelical charismatic theology.

I was baptized in the Kirkwall Baptist Church by the pastor, the Rev. Ken Denman, on Sunday the 24th January 1965 and received into membership one week later, on Sunday the 31st January, one day after my sixteenth birthday. I became a member before celebrating, for the first time, the Lord's Supper. Both my baptism and the celebration of the Lord's Supper were special then, and more so now. The Communion service is my "favourite" worship service each week and it is a privilege to remember Christ's death on the cross for the likes of me. I inevitably thank the Lord in my heart that I am His forever and that He has forgiven all my sins.

I wish to record also that Pastor Ken Denman's ministry had a lasting effect on me during my teenage years. I particularly remember his series of sermons from 1 Corinthians. I loved the idea of such systematic Bible preaching and when, later in the Birmingham Bible Institute, I studied the same Scripture, I received my highest mark (98%). Something had stuck! The Rev Ken McNeish, and his wife Sisel, followed Pastor Denman and their pastoral ministry was second to none. Pastor McNeish encouraged me on my journey into Bible College. Jeannie and I became very fond of the Rev Francis Gordon and his wife Kay. We got to know them on our first furlough from Peru in 1978. Both Francis and Kay were just such fine people. They served the Kirkwall Baptist Church for more than two decades. Indeed, my home church, and folk in it (many family relatives), played an important role in my journey through life.

I felt the call of God on my life to be a missionary in Peru soon after my conversion to Christ. What I remember is that a missionary called Bill Speed, of the Evangelical Union of South America (EUSA), spoke in the recently formed Baptist Church in Kirkwall, Orkney (my parents were among the founding members in 1959), of his missionary work in Peru. I was hooked and from that moment did not vacillate in believing that God had spoken to me in my heart. Others at my schools (Harray Public School, 1954–1961, and Stromness Academy, 1961–1966) outlined their secular professions-to-be, while I held to my intention to be a missionary in Peru.

Two of the happiest years of my life came after finishing my Higher Grade studies in 1966 (English, Geography, Engineering Drawing and Woodwork) when I worked with my older brothers, Ivan and Robert, on the family farm, along with other farm employees. I enjoyed working alongside them and sometimes with my father there too. I have the utmost respect for farmers and for my brothers. I wonder if, as part of a big family, it was there that I learned (and still am learning) not to be envious. I count it a privilege to have grown up on a big farm and now I am also glad that there were farm chores after school, during school holidays and at weekends. Those activities were formative on my character and helped developed some muscle!

My father had always known how to find chores for his tribe of boys, and I did not always like his timing. I have one vivid memory of when I was the oldest sibling at my primary school, probably ten or eleven years of age. In the winter months my father would come, ostensibly to pick me up, with our open back, long wheel-based Land Rover loaded down with silage. The idea was for me to accompany him after school the seven miles away from the family farm to where he was wintering cattle outside. My task was to drive the vehicle while he forked out the feed. On one occasion I was hungry and tired and just wanted to get home, so I ran out of classes and began to take a shortcut home across some fields when I heard (the horn) and saw him appear. I can tell you, when he successfully summoned me back, I knew I would never repeat another attempt at a great escape. Incidentally, my sister Doreen (three years younger) did not get picked up. She walked the one and a half miles home in the cold.

I have to admit that, while my older two brothers, mentioned above, were born farmers with a great eye for quality sheep and cattle, and pedigree animal breeding, I just enjoyed working and, in particular, walking around fields to make sure the sheep were O.K. What a great task it was! I learned to deepen my prayer life as I walked and distinctly remember, at eighteen years of age, asking for the first time, that God fill me with His Holy Spirit. I know God met with me.

I think that, as the younger sibling, I was given the pigs to feed and the pigsties to clean out. It was a smelly task. Nevertheless, it was there that I learned from my father's example of work that I should not ask anyone else to do what I was not prepared to do myself. This I would later take to Peru with me when I went as a young and very green missionary.

Map of Peru

1
Bible College and Pre-Peru
1968–1973

*"Any work of God of eternal value demands
a long obedience in the same direction."*

It was in October 1968 that I began my studies in the now non-existent Birmingham Bible Institute[2] located in Edgbaston, Birmingham. At nineteen years of age, I was the youngest among a student body of over 100. All were enrolled with a view to train for Christian ministry, either at home or overseas. At that time, Bible Colleges did not like to accept students straight from school. My rather sheltered Orcadian upbringing was exposed to a multicultural city. Besides, College life each day was regimented by house prayers at 6.30am, followed by personal devotions, chores, breakfast, classes, lunch, some more classes, and controlled study between 6.30–9.30pm. Lights had to be out by 10.30pm.

Weekends were devoted to evangelistic outreach and, for some reason, I was assigned to open air speaking in the Bull Ring at the centre of Birmingham and then for almost two years as leader of an outreach team to children. I confess that the activity I least enjoyed was to reach into Clubs and Discotheques. I was always uncomfortable there, never settled to the atmosphere and loud music seemed to paralyse my brain. I have had an aversion to the same ever since!

As time passed, I found that I was often asked to preach in different churches at the weekend. The College was going through quite a pronounced Pentecostal phase, although there was also a group of students who adhered to a version of John Wesley's teaching on entire sanctification. I mention that because, although I went through a Pentecostal preference of my own, I was, apparently, viewed as "safe" and trusted to be sensible in preaching. Indeed, I remember several memorable experiences where people responded to sermons and came to Christ. More than once I recall the need to "enable" people to receive Christ. Others call this "deliverance", but I prefer to share the events carefully.

It was a joy to meet students such as Chris Papworth and May Walker who were also headed to Peru and were in contact with what was then called the Regions

---

2   Several other Bible Colleges in the UK have ceased to exist since then, often due to becoming economically non-viable.

Beyond Missionary Union (RBMU, later Latin Link). They both served for a time in Peru on church planting teams, as did I when I went there. It was while at College that I decided to go to Peru with RBMU. Also while at College, I developed an interdenominational ethos as I attended different churches. The pastor (London Bible College trained) in Selly Park Baptist always delivered a doctrinally sound sermon. When free, I would visit Selly Oak Elim Church and loved Pastor Capel's succinct Gospel preaching (usually no more than fifteen minutes) and the resulting response. During my last year at College I regularly chose Graham Street Elim Church, where in practically every sermon Pastor Coles exuded his pastoral ministry. I invariably came away blessed, encouraged in my faith and in my relationship to Christ. Those were formative experiences that helped me appreciate the rich diversity in the Church.

Studies were demanding, activities tiring, and it was not until my third year that I really applied myself to study. I freely confess, with the help of hindsight, that some young men, like me, take longer to mature than young ladies! Indeed, my last year set a pattern that was later to become part of my life. I studied both College courses and for a University of London external qualification and graduated in June 1971. I have always treasured my BBI Diploma, awarded with distinction, as representing a shift in my commitment to study. I remember that Tom Rees preached powerfully at the graduation service.

During the Summer after graduation I was "employed" (not for the first time) by BBI as a handyman, led a children's campaign in an Elim Church and a youth camp from a Brethren Assembly in Birmingham, near to Snowdonia in Wales, where a number of young people came to Christ. I was again confronted by the need to pray, along with elder Roy Fellows (a schoolteacher) from the Brethren Assembly in Birmingham, and ask the Lord to rebuke demonic activity in the life of one young man who had been paralysed by fear after dabbling in the occult. The Lord set him free!

It was in July of 1971 that I also visited Northern Ireland for the first time. There was much unrest at that time and I witnessed the military presence in Belfast. Besides preaching on the streets, I took part in a march on July 12th! I was invited to hear Dr Ian Paisley preach in his church on Sunday. I admit I was in awe of his physical presence and style as he entered the pulpit and observed the congregation. In fact, I remember his text and its delivery—"The flesh profiteth nothing"—but could not for the life of me understand how in his sermon he interpreted this to mean "the outward trappings of the Catholic Church". Nor did I appreciate how he developed his theme from the text to make the assertion that "they [the Catholics] believe you receive grace through your stomach". I understood this to be a reference to the Mass but have never been convinced that the pulpit should be used to attack something that is sacred to so many.

On returning to Orkney, several friends from College and I led an outreach campaign in the Dounby United Free (UF) Church of Scotland. Afterwards I was asked to be their pastor. Incidentally, before my parents were part of the new Baptist Church in Kirkwall in 1959, we had been taken faithfully as children to the Dounby UF Church. Our family doctor, Dr Emslie, was their acting pastor. So it was that I sought to serve the Dounby UF Church for the following year and a half. As a non-ordained pastor, and as a Baptist, I was content to allow an ordained UF minister (either from Shetland or Scotland) to lead the Lord's Supper or baptise every few months. As I stayed with my parents, I was asked to do my walking and "sheep watching" in lieu of rent. Indeed, it was during that time that I purchased my first car, a second-hand white VW Beetle. I revelled in being back on home turf and in checking the sheep as I drove on the runways of part of a World War II aerodrome that my father had bought. I also managed to purchase my first ever tape recorder! Ah, such fond memories!

I have similar memories of making friends in the church in Dounby and remember fishing off the western coast of Birsay, Orkney, along with John Velzian. We spent whole days in a dinghy catching haddock. We threw the mackerel back in at John's instructions, as they tangled the lines and, anyway, they had a strong taste. How things change! I came to know and appreciate two Jim Stockans, one of whom, without either of us realising it, mentored me. He was a godly Christian businessman who made oatcakes. I still buy them—they are the best! I am sure that many visits to his house, which always ended in prayer, were probably insensitive intrusions of a young man. Jim's godly wife May was always welcoming. Jim had a way of repeating things! For instance, I learned, and cannot forget, that "the glory must always be for the Lord because the Lord does not share His glory". I also remember him often repeating: "Ken, if you are ever accused and are guilty, hands up to the Lord. If you are not guilty as accused, hands up to the Lord!" How could I forget that? I have had to practise both approaches many times!

During my time back in Orkney, I arranged for a return visit in 1972 of my good Welsh friend Alan Penduck. Along with young folk from Dounby and the Kirkwall Baptist Church, we went to the Youth Hostel on the island of Hoy for a Christian Camp. It was during that time that one night, after our devotional session, the older young people, some leaders, Alan and I met for prayer. I remember I decided that instead of just listening to Alan's talks, it would be good to ask God to meet us and bless us.

What followed left me as a spectator! From the first moment God moved and, although folk asked me to pray with/for them, I knew and still know, that God was moving by His Spirit. I remember my younger brother Martin's prayer for God to bless. Jim Stockan's (my mentor) daughter Anne immediately followed in clear praise to God. Others started to worship the Lord spontaneously and we all continued well into the morning. Some had so used their voices that they were hoarse! Alan and I finally took a stroll in the moonlight before dawn to contemplate what I believe to this day was a mighty mini-movement of God. Several of those present that night later went into Christian ministry, including both mentioned above. I certainly gave, and give, God the glory for what He did. I know I did not do it! Aye, the glory is His.

2
Costa Rica
1973–1974

"Trust in the Lord with all your heart…"
Proverbs 3:5a

During the pastorate in Orkney, I was in touch with RBMU and applied to the Mission. After being interviewed by the Scottish Council, it was recommended that I have more experience and so it was that I left Orkney towards the end of 1972 to serve as Assistant Pastor to the Rev. Gilbert Ritchie, in what was then Stenhouse Baptist Church in Edinburgh. During that time, I was privileged to stay in Currie with my oldest brother Tom, his first wife Mary and their two small daughters, Jean and Rosemary.

I suppose, if I am honest, I was disappointed to leave Orkney so soon and for being asked to deepen my experience of ministry. With hindsight, I am sure that those who made that decision knew I was in need of much more preparation. Indeed, Gilbert Ritchie enabled me to reflect on different aspects of personal discipline. His wisdom in drawing my attention to my dislike for committees was timely, but I confess that I have always had to fight the temptation to be a loner, and committees were to become a part of my life that later led me into the joys of administration!

Not only so, but while my departure to Costa Rica for Spanish language was delayed by several months, on the other side of the Atlantic, Jeannie Yoder's departure from Delaware to Costa Rica was accelerated by several months. In God's providence we were to meet for the first time on a bus in San José in October of 1973.

Before I left for Costa Rica on the 1st May 1973, financial support had to be raised and that came in from people in the Baptist churches in Westray and Kirkwall, and the Dounby UF Church. I remember clearly that full support was £600/year! I also remember that in Costa Rica I was given the princely sum of £40/month and, of that, I had to pay the Costa Rican family with whom I stayed, £32.50p/month. I therefore had £7.50 in local currency for all other expenses. Although I had had to trust the Lord along the way before, this opened up opportunities to grow in my faith in the Lord in a new way.

I revelled in language study and the little French that remained in my brain from studies in Stromness Academy soon left me completely. Each day started with fresh bread, a boiled egg and fresh filter coffee with hot milk. It helped that the man of the house was employed as a coffee taster. I travelled to and from *El*

Instituto de Lengua Española squeezed onto a bus, then back for a lunch in my Costa Rican "home" for the national staple of rice and beans. I progressed in my language studies because I was both motivated and had many opportunities to practise each day.

I remember that I first saw Jeannie on a bus on the way to classes when I was introduced to her by Rose King, another American Mennonite language student. Jeannie did not join in the conversation, so I wanted to include her. The first thing I ever said to her, besides the initial greeting was—"Would you like to trim my moustache?" What a clonk I was! Nevertheless, and despite that embarrassing beginning, let me cut to the chase.

I began to think she was quite something and, over the ensuing month or two, we chatted sensibly and met at Bible studies for single Spanish language students. Shortly before Christmas, I was getting serious about her in my mind. I had even shared this with an American friend Phil Banta, another missionary candidate and student, who constantly encouraged me to ask her out. To be honest, I was scared in the face of such imponderables. Sufficient to state that I had had a couple of friendships before that had led up *cul-de-sacs*. On the basis of that, I had promised the Lord when I was 22 that I would not start another relationship until I was sure I would marry that person. Further, and since arriving in Costa Rica, I'd had so many approaches (almost on a daily basis) from Costa Rican ladies. Yes, that really happened and I knew that had never been the pattern back home! So, while keeping my promise to the Lord, I had to be sure not to start something I could not finish.

As the winter semester came to an end in the language school, Jeannie informed me that she would be going out to some village along with other Mennonites to do outreach. By this stage I just wanted to get to know her better, so I turned to the Lord, in my weak faith, to ask three things. Do not do this at home! Firstly, I prayed that if there could be a future (marriage) in the relationship, that Jeannie would come to the church I attended on Sunday and sit by me. That had never happened. Secondly, I asked that the projected outreach would be called off. Thirdly, I asked in all earnestness, that Jeannie would bring up matters of the heart. My prayers were from the heart. I needed guidance.

The next Sunday while seated in my church trying to decipher the language in my Spanish Bible, I was aware that someone had sat down next to me. It was Jeannie and, I confess, my heart missed a few beats. After the service she invited me to the Mennonite House for lunch. As we travelled there on the bus, she informed me of the cancelled trip to the villages. I believe in God's providence and my heart (my blood pump) was responding along with my heart! When we arrived at the central building for lunch, there was no one there. They came later. So it was that Jeannie brought up the matters of the heart and asked me directly what my intentions were. We talked.

Of course, that didn't settle anything and she sort of liked someone else—an ugly brute he was too! Did I write that I did not suffer from jealousy? I had been asked by an American couple to look after a house on the outskirts of San José for another couple. However, my own wish by this stage was to get to know who Jeannie was. We had discovered that we shared the same faith, had been brought up in similar, but different, backgrounds, so I begged off staying in the missionary house although I would have been paid generously for it.

Jeannie and I had a few weeks of what used to be called courting. We moved to the topic of marriage quite quickly and I had suggested an engagement ring, to which Jeannie retorted that her Mennonite church (Conservative Mennonite Conference) did not approve of such "outward adornment". I really had no idea what I was getting into. In my youthful enthusiasm I asked whether, if I prayed for a specific sum of money and the prayer was answered, she would accept the offer. The sum of money I agreed on was £45. I guess my faith was weak and stingy! Actually, that seemed a lot of money to me at the time. Again, do not do this at home! So it was that, meanwhile, the Scottish Council had agreed to send each Scottish RBMU missionary the sum of £45. Within days I was informed that money would be forthcoming. With that news I ran to Jeannie's house about a kilometre from my own house to tell her.

We were doing a lot of walking and chatting. I missed so many meals that I soon lost weight and, I confess, was missing early classes due to too many late nights chatting either in the front room in her house or in mine. It was in February 1974 that Jeannie was told that her father, then 68 years of age, was dying of cancer. He had been operated on 13 years before and had had his stomach removed. By then Jeannie and I were definitely in love and she asked me to accompany her to her home in Delaware in the USA for the funeral. I had no money! Nevertheless, Jeannie's mission offered to loan me the money and for me to pay them back on my return to Costa Rica. Ah, I made these decisions without reference to folk in RBMU! More of that later!

Nothing prepared me for the world I was about to enter. We left Costa Rica together for her Dad's funeral on 18th February 1974. Jeannie and I were picked up at the airport by her nephew Ronnie and her brother Doyle, who, with his six foot four inch frame promptly "fell on my neck and kissed me". We were taken directly to the "viewing", before which Jeannie had put up her hair and had taken out her "head covering". After meeting Jeannie's oldest brother Samuel (in a grey sports jacket with an open necked shirt) and his wife Effie, I was immediately aware of men in plain black suits and in what appeared to me to be clerical collars. After a query about all the clergy present Jeannie clarified that many Mennonites dressed that way.

Thereafter, I was on a steep learning curve as I met siblings, their spouses and extended family and the Mennonite community at the funeral. I attended Greenwood Mennonite Church on Sunday along with Jeannie. As we lined up to enter, I became aware of the men greeting Bishop John Mishler with a kiss on the lips. I immediately asked Jeannie what that was. She replied: "Ah, that is the holy kiss", to which I remember that I replied, "There is nothing holy about that!" I made sure my right hand was extended and my left clenched when I greeted Bishop John! He always showed us true friendship and no holy kiss.

After visiting a few jewellery shops, and with prices starting at $350 I managed to buy Jeannie a ring for the princely sum of £45 ($100 at the time). After all, isn't a ring just a symbol? It was hard to leave Jeannie in the USA. Her mission agreed she should not return to Costa Rica as no teaching post had become available for her. Anyway, she and I were planning a future together. On return to San José someone had sent a cheque, without me telling anyone, for the amount I owed for my fare. I was grateful to Jeannie's bosses for their trust in me.

So it was that I finished out my studies in Costa Rica as we continued our courtship apart and my letter writing skills increased as I penned one each day to Jeannie for the next nine months. Jeannie and I had set our wedding date for the 28th September, and with that in my mind and oblivious to what lay ahead, I headed out to Lima, Peru on the 20th April 1974.

3
Abancay, Apurímac
1974

"Do not depend on your own understanding…"
Proverbs 3:5b

On arrival in Jorge Chávez Airport in Lima on the 20th April 1974, a lady in an elegant dress and immaculate hairdo, with a US southern drawl, asked me if I was Ken Scott. After acknowledging the fact, I asked how she had guessed, to which she replied: "You look British!" I never knew what that meant especially as the plaid jacket I wore was bought in the USA and given to me by Jeannie. Ah, those were different times! I suppose that with hair covering my ears, a moustache, flared hipster trousers and a fitted jacket with lapels as broad as my shoulders I stood out from any American young man. I noticed thereafter that many American men at that time wore their trousers a couple of inches above their shoes.

The lady was Dotty Battle and she announced that we needed to wait for Malone. I asked who Malone was and she replied that she called him Malone, whereas others knew him as Cooper Battle. They were American missionaries in RBMU and Cooper was the man in Lima who took care of administration. My first impression of Malone/Cooper was of a not-so-immaculate husband, whose trousers were hanging down over a protruding tummy, jacket hanging off his shoulders, with glasses poised on the point of his nose and who was talking to himself. His trousers scuffed the ground! Without any introduction he gave the order: "Scott, get in!" Silence ensued as I sat in the back seat of his double cabin pickup. He spoke in English (I think) only to Dotty as we travelled, and I cannot remember if I understood anything. On arrival at their home, I was invited to sit down. Cooper then announced: "I do not like Pentecostals." I remember stating that I was not Pentecostal. I feel I have had to clarify this many times since to many different people. Ah well, anyway, I came to quite like Cooper, in time.

The next day I was given instructions by Cooper to get on a certain bus and to get off at *"migraciones"* (immigration offices) and to present my documents along with other papers given to me by him. I did ask for some more clarification about landmarks and, to this day, I do not know how I managed. I also remember instructions that on return I should help in Cooper's print shop. I got on well with the young Peruvian who worked for him. Unfortunately, I cannot remember his name. After a lapse of a few days, I was sent on the bus daily to enquire after progress on the visa and then to work in the print shop. I confess that, besides being attentive on each trip, I asked the Lord to help me not get lost. I remember that I was having a lot of stomach trouble on arrival from Costa Rica with all the ensuing delicate risks! This continued for some years in Peru. More of that later. Nevertheless, I was finally to be given my non-immigrant resident visa on the 14th of May.

I need to interrupt my flow here because I remember visiting a Christian and Missionary Alliance Church in Lima in 1974, days after arrival in Peru as a new missionary. What I witnessed changed my life. The local church was experiencing phenomenal growth and blessings. It was self-governing, self-propagating and self-supporting, with a discipleship programme I have seldom seen duplicated. The experience led to a steep learning curve. Any thoughts of self-importance or self-interest as a missionary were overtaken by the glory of God in action and the need to be humble as a result. I took that memory, and the image of Peruvians in church leadership, into ministry. It would take longer for me to implement it.

To return to the story, before I had my Peruvian identity booklet (*Carnet de Identidad*) in my hand, I stumped up for a plane fare to Cuzco. I had been delegated by Field Council to work alongside College friend Chris Papworth in Abancay, the capital city of the department of Apurímac. So it was that I travelled to Cuzco, the ancient capital of the Inca Empire located in the Andes mountain range. All my documents, including my passport, were in *"migraciones"* in Lima. In Cuzco I followed the instructions I had been given and purchased a ticket on a bus. I arrived in Abancay about 4.00am, after a ten-hour journey over rough roads, much later than expected, and was relieved to be welcomed by Chris who had waited up. I had been careful to only drink Coca Cola and eat soup *en route*.

It was good to have reached my destination and to meet the Apurímac team soon afterwards. At that time Cherry (Susana) Noble and Jackie (Anita) Howe (later to marry Chris) worked in Antabamba, at least eight hours away over rough roads while Rosemary Flack and Jessie Norton (a veteran missionary who came out of retirement to accompany Rosemary) were in Chalhuanca, over three hours away by road. Chris had served overseas before with Operation Mobilisation, including a lengthy stint in India. Stewart and Jan McIntosh were on furlough in the UK with their four children at that time. Indeed, they were all more experienced in a cross-cultural setting than me.

Chris had worked before in Abancay with the McIntoshes and I was keen to learn. A pattern for ministry was soon established whereby we travelled to other villages on evangelistic trips as well as ministering to the small group in Abancay. A team of short-term volunteers from the USA and Canada (Project Timothy) joined us for a few months, as well as a team of Peruvian students from the Lima Evangelical Seminary at another time. Chris was a good organiser and there was much to learn.

I do remember travelling on foot to a village or two (Vito and Antilla) with Bryan Twedell from Canada. We took very little with us and sought accommodation, as did other teams, in the villages. We were mistaken for priests in Vito, despite efforts to explain otherwise, and were given accommodation and mention was made of Mass in the morning. As we were settling in for the night, an attractive lady was brought to our room by the village leaders and it was clear what was on offer. We politely declined and the next morning explained again that we were *"evangélicos"* and not priests. Nevertheless, we were asked to present the Gospel and we left literature.

Jeannie had made application, after my departure from the USA, to the American branch of RBMU in Philadelphia. She was duly accepted as a missionary candidate and began to raise support. Jeannie and I had presented our plans to get married on the 28th September 1974 in Delaware. However, while the Council in the US gave the green light, the RBMU Field Council in Peru informed us in August 1974 that they did not approve our request. The RBMU Peru Field Director, Ole Sorell and his wife Vera, along with Chris, brought the Field Council decision back to Abancay regarding our marriage plans. Ole and Vera were Canadians and I confess I warmed to them both from that time. Jeannie and I moved the wedding date, with (albeit reluctant) approval, to the 28th December 1974.

Ernest Oliver was General Secretary of the UK RBMU and he wrote explaining that in his case (a missionary in India for two decades), and in that of other missionaries, those who intended marriage had been required to spend a missionary term (four years) apart on the "field" before being allowed to marry. They were certainly made of sterner stuff! To be fair, I was reprimanded for not informing the folk in London about my friendship with Jeannie until after I had travelled to the US and back. I remember that my head had gone away with my heart and my class marks and attendance dipped. The evidence was in the report sent by the Language Institute to the office in London.

Nevertheless, we were allowed to marry in December provided that we would serve a total of eight years in Peru, i.e. five years in my case and three for Jeannie, before a first furlough and return home for either of us. Jeannie was asked by the Mission, in lieu of not having Bible College training, to complete the Scofield Bible correspondence course offered by Moody Bible Institute. I had even tried, unsuccessfully, to phone Jeannie from Abancay for eight hours one day to relay all the conditions set for us. Jeannie and I did finally understand the conditions stipulated after several letters had crossed over.

I will never forget my first RBMU Field Conference at the end of November 1974 in a Southern Baptist Mission Centre in Chaclacayo, outside Lima. By that time I had begun to realise that the American and UK missionary contingents had had different opinions for some time regarding the relationship between the Mission and Peruvian denominations, and also in regard to the understanding and acceptability of Pentecostal doctrine and practice. The penny finally dropped with me when I met two RBMU North American missionaries for the first time. At Conference we three had just washed our hands in the bathroom when, without a handshake being offered, or introductions being made, I was challenged about my beliefs regarding the Holy Spirit. I was asked directly whether I had ever lost control and been thrown to the floor at any time. I believe that I replied graciously (on the outside), without even trying to explain my beliefs, that when God deigned to bless me, as in any case, I had never been more in control of my faculties. *Déjà vu.*

4
Our Wedding
1974

*"Seek his will in all you do,
and he will show you which path to take."*
Proverbs 3:6a

I travelled to the USA on the 7th December 1974 and honestly answered the questions posed by the immigration officer that I was entering the United States in order to get married. I had been assured in Lima that I needed no special visa to enter the country. The officer asked me for my "boyfriend's visa". I was detained for several hours under armed guard and then questioned by a Spanish speaking lady officer. After giving assurances that my money came from the UK, things changed for the better. I did not mention that my field monthly allowance was by then the princely sum of £25. It was after I stated that I intended to return to Peru, with my bride after marriage, that I was allowed entrance. Methinks it would not be as easy now.

Once in Delaware things were easier. Jeannie and I had to have medical tests—a requirement in the USA to make sure a couple carried no STDs into marriage—before we applied for our marriage licence in Georgetown, Delaware. It was a time of getting to know Jeannie's family and for them to know me. As already mentioned, I was the first non-Mennonite to marry in Greenwood Mennonite Church. Bishop John Mishler was instrumental in this. Of course, it is worth mentioning that most girls who married "out" usually married those who did not profess faith in Christ. Therefore, this led traditionally to "banning" and "shunning". Jeannie's parents had both been members of the Amish community in their earlier days. Greenwood Mennonite Church, on the other hand, belonged to an evangelical Mennonite Conference. Sufficient to state that different Mennonite churches varied in their application and adherence to rules, as I was to discover.

Our wedding was on the 28th December 1974 and Joe Conley, the US Director of RBMU, preached the sermon. He had been most helpful in facilitating Jeannie's application and acceptance into the Mission. Due to the Peru RBMU Field Executive's late decision in rejecting our request to marry on the 28th September, none of my family was present. That is another story. I remember being nervous. Actually, I have never been more nervous in my life. I believed/believe that marriage is for life and I was filled with awe, anticipation and joy as I repeated my memorised vows.

I certainly felt married and that I had passed through a holy rite of passage. The Mennonites consider marriage as one of seven holy ordinances. It was a great day and in the afternoon all the several hundred guests sat down with us to a meal prepared and supplied by Greenwood Mennonite Church. Jeannie and I were both penniless. As I remember it Jeannie had made her own wedding dress and the cake. Then she was broke! Jeannie's mother Lena gave us a wedding present of a night in a Howard Johnson's Motel along our route to our honeymoon in West Virginia. Indeed, neither Jeannie nor I understood that breakfast was included in the price. This meant we waited quite a while the next morning to be served and had to pay extra and, of course, the tip! We drove in a car loaned by Jeannie's mother's new husband Albert and spent our honeymoon in a luxurious log cabin in West Virginia, loaned to us by Jeannie's Uncle Glen (one of her mother's younger brothers). It was there that we met more family, all Mennonites, and some of the finest people I had ever met.

5
Chalhuanca
1975–1978

*"The will of God in the present is invariably messy –
it is only pleasant in retrospect."*

Before we both arrived in Peru on the 1st March 1975, there were things to be done. Our marriage certificate first had to be signed by the Secretary of State of Delaware, then by a representative of the Secretary of State of the United States (Henry Kissinger!) and finally legally translated into Spanish. I was asked to speak on a few occasions, did some construction work alongside a crew of Mennonite hunks and more with Jeannie's new stepfather. I also prepared wooden crates in which we packed Jeannie's belongings and some wedding gifts. The crates made the journey along with us as air freight. Although we were charged for their transport in the US airport, they were "miraculously" cleared in Jorge Chávez Airport in Lima at no cost.

Having gone through the bureaucratic documentation process myself in 1974, I was there to accompany Jeannie on her journey. Of course, we also had to register as a couple. Jeannie and I had been assigned by the Field Executive to work in church planting in Chalhuanca and so we travelled to the Andes via Cuzco. We did not travel until Jeannie had her Peruvian documents. The bus journey from Cuzco was long, delayed and arduous and, in my zeal to avoid stomach complications, we only ate a chocolate bar (infamous *"sublime"* in Peru) during its duration. It was the rainy season and there were landslides. The McIntoshes (Stewart and Jan with their four children—Alison, John, Ruth and Rachel) were back in Peru and were stranded in Chalhuanca due to landslides. Stewart came through to Abancay and we eventually were cleared to travel to Chalhuanca.

Rosemary Flack was on furlough and had loaned us her pickup until she returned. No amount of missionary orientation prepared Jeannie or me for what was to come over the next three years (1975–1978). Abancay (capital of the Department of Apurímac and of the Province of Abancay) nestled in the mountains at about 2,200 metres while Chalhuanca (capital of the Province of Aymaraes in the Department of Apurímac) sat alongside a river at over 2,800 metres. It was possible to travel from Lima via Ica, Nazca, Puquio and, eventually, Chalhuanca, before travelling on to Abancay and other destinations like Cuzco. Cuzco was to become a haven for us in the ensuing years.

Jeannie had come to this point from the relative comfort of Delaware, to what was then known as a Third World[3] country, to its capital city of Lima to Cuzco, Abancay, and that first journey along dirt roads to Chalhuanca. We had been told that a Christian sister called Felícitas would be waiting for us on our journey in a small *adobe* house some kilometres before arrival in Chalhuanca. She had prepared us a meal. So it was that we finished our soup and were then offered boiled potatoes and cheese. The basic rule we have always followed is that if it is boiled and cooked it is safe. The cheese was not quite on the same level. Felícitas reached for her store of cheese from the smoky rafters and broke off small hard pieces of musty, discoloured bits infiltrated with "stuff". The potatoes were carefully peeled and eaten, then when our dear sister Felícitas retreated to her smoky "kitchen" with its open wood fire, I surreptitiously accepted Jeannie's protein and kept it for "later" in my jacket pocket! On noticing that we had "finished" our cheese we were given more—a basic rule of hospitality in the mountains of Peru.

At this point I believe it appropriate for Jeannie to tell of her own Chalhuanca experience (1975–78):

> *Chalhuanca was a small rural town high in the Andes of South Peru. If you saw it from a distance it could look idyllic!! Situated in a valley with a river running beside the town, the road to Lima was its main street and buses to and from the capital city stopped in Chalhuanca to allow passengers to rest-stop.*
>
> *But it was a primitive place in many ways. All roads and streets were dirt. The electricity supply was limited and sporadic. Toilet facilities were either in the small restaurants or in the streets and food was very basic.*
>
> *Ken had been in Peru for about 9 months before he came to the USA to get married and had rented a few rooms in a house in the street parallel to the main street. I arrived, a new bride, in March 1975 to this small town. The Mission placed us in this "strategic" town to plant a church.*
>
> *I should state, rightly or wrongly, that I never considered myself a "missionary". I was "called" to be Ken's wife: where he went, I went, and I would be a support to him.*
>
> *Chalhuanca was lovely early in the morning—clear, bright and cold! There was a smell of freshly baked bread in the mornings also. Unfortunately, this did not mask the smell of urine just outside our front door. We named our street "Pee Street"—to this day, if I see a man facing a wall, I avert my eyes!! They would boldly greet you with a "good morning" while doing their thing!*
>
> *Food, and the lack of it, is a vivid memory. In the very early weeks of our time in Chalhuanca I had a pressure cooker and a primus stove—one ring! And there were more burnt meals than not! Ken and I, and a single lady missionary*

---

3 This vocabulary is unacceptable today. Indeed, Peru is as sophisticated as many western countries and perhaps "majority world" would be more suitable terminology to use in our milieu in 2019.

(Rosemary Flack), were the only ex-pats in town and she was going on furlough, so she gave us the use of her two-ring gas cooker.

I thought I knew how to cook as I was raised in a large family in the USA and had been preparing meals since my teen years. Meat and two veg—not a problem—with a homemade sweet to follow! But there was no supermarket. Indeed, no market of any kind! No meat! Well, that is another story. What was sold was in the doorway of someone's house—onions, potatoes, sometimes a carrot or beetroot. Most of what I saw I did not recognise, much less, know how to cook.

Potatoes became our staple diet and even some of them were unfamiliar—pink and purple and knobbly. And not many weeks into our time in Chalhuanca I realised I was pregnant. Nausea was a constant reality, which did not help with food—I couldn't face it, never mind cook it.

Meat was a challenge in every way—getting it, preparing it and eating it! But I had to do it! Up at 5am—to the place they sold it and into the queue! Open at 7am and a rush to get a place. One kilo was allowed—bone and meat—shattered bone and wood splinters from the tree stump where axe-wielding women did their thing. Sometimes only one skinny beast had been killed and everything would run out before it arrived at my turn. I felt almost relief—but what to cook instead?

If I was fortunate enough to get a kilo of bone and meat, I took it home and picked through the meat to get out the shattered bone and wood splinters, washed it as well as I could, placed it in the pressure cooker and hoped it would be edible! Months passed when there was no meat because the cattle were too thin. It was a question of simply waiting for the rainy season and for the grass to grow enough to fatten the cattle.

Ken and I did not know each other when we got married. Of course, as Ken has related, it was not an arranged marriage—well, not by our parents anyway. We met at Language School in Costa Rica. I was there to teach for two years and then was to return to the USA and to my teaching career. Ken was learning Spanish on his way to Peru. We had our first romantic outing at the end of December 1973 (as related by Ken) and two weeks later we knew we would marry.

The job I was to have in January 1974 never materialised and my father died in February 1974. A huge question loomed in my mind. How could this work? Ken was from Scotland—Orkney. (I did not know where Orkney was—I hardly knew where Scotland was!) I was from the USA and had a commitment to my Mission in Costa Rica for two years. Ken was on his way to Peru etc, etc.

The job did not materialise, my father died in February and my Mission released me from my commitment and gave its blessing on our marriage. Ken has already told the part where he travelled to the USA with me for my father's funeral and met my family. We got engaged and he returned to Costa Rica to finish his language studies and on to Peru. Our nine months of separation in 1974 were spent in writing letters. There were no phone connections, no social *media and no "face" time. Letters took three weeks to arrive and then three weeks back.*

This was not the recommended way to get to know someone. It was during that time that I applied to the US part of RBMU and set about raising support. We planned a simple wedding and so it was that we married at the end of December 1974 and travelled to Peru together on March 1st, 1975.

We got to know each other in Chalhuanca. There was no one else in our small town to speak English to and certainly no interfering in-laws! We were 10 hours from the nearest airport and 30 hours from Lima. We well and truly had to work it out. But I missed my family!! I think I cried every day of that first three-year term on the field.

I look back on those early years and think that modern mission workers probably would have demanded more training, more commodities, more support. We did not know any different. We were instructed to go and do, and that is what we did. At the time it was a day-at-a-time, doing what needed to be done and trying to build friendships that would be to God's glory. People were suspicious and spread the rumour that we were really CIA agents!!!! It was not easy to gain their confidence. For me it was difficult as the women spoke mainly in Quechua. Nevertheless, we did have a small growing group of believers.

I can imagine that Jeannie's account of the axe-wielding meat ladies in Chalhuanca may well raise the issue for any reader of why I had not entered into that fray. The truth is that I did go sometimes but it was a woman's world. One younger axe woman seemed always to think she was doing me a favour by including the knee joint and shin bone. Aaaggghhh! I think the idea was that the marrow would make nice soup and I remember one meatless three-month period. Jeannie prepared potatoes in many different ways, and it is a tribute to her that we still love eating them. It is good to remember that potatoes were first discovered in Peru by Sir Francis Raleigh! Where would we in the West be without them!

Regarding Jeannie's comment on people suspecting us of being CIA agents, as ridiculous as the idea might have been, it was a current that permeated the country at a wider level. Such rumours were not restricted to our location, but similar reports came to us from missionaries in other parts of Peru. We could never imagine what it might be that was of such strategic importance in a remote town in the Andes like Chalhuanca. On one occasion, a shopkeeper even asked Jeannie what our "real mission" in the town was. If I had had any doubts about what some thought of us, it was dispelled when I produced my camera to take some photographs of a protest march against the government of about a hundred secondary school students in the town. As I proceeded to take a couple of photographs, I became aware, firstly, that missiles, mostly stones, were being thrown at me and secondly, above the noise, shouts of "spy", "CIA", "death to the gringo" and more, reached my ears. I made a deliberate retreat to our house. We later discovered from students known to us that several left-wing orientated teachers had organised the march and had "allowed" students to participate. After that, I learned to be careful in taking photographs.

Our three years in Chalhuanca placed us on a steep learning curve. Cultural issues played their part as did political change in Peru. My stories will not major on socio-political changes but there is no doubt that the bigger picture impinged on the realities that surrounded us. General Juan Velasco Alvarado, under the title of the First President of the Revolutionary Government of the Armed Forces of Peru, had seized power from President Fernando Belaúnde Terry (1963–68) on the 3rd October 1968 in what was a bloodless military coup. Left-wing President Velasco was close to the rank and file of Peruvians. His ill-fated reforms drew support through intentional declarations such as follows: "Farmer, the landowner will never again feed off your poverty."

Soon after our arrival in Chalhuanca, General Francisco Morales Bermúdez seized power to become the Second President of the Revolutionary Government of the Armed Forces of Peru. President Morales was sworn into office from the 30th August 1975 until the 28th July 1980[4]. His avowed intention was to counter the left socialist leanings of Velasco and he proclaimed a "second phase" that would lead to a return to democracy. In truth, the country was in a severe economic crisis that continued during his presidency and by April 1980, Peru's economy was in deep depression. All who lived in Peru during those years experienced the knock-on effects.

Our Chalhuanca years were hard for us both. Mixed with our "culture shock", as illustrated from Jeannie's perspective above, we had many new experiences and times of great joy. I had left Jeannie in the Evangelical Union of South America's renowned Clinic in Urcos (beyond Cuzco) in October 1975 in the capable care of Dr Nat and Doreen Davies, anticipating her giving birth in late November. In the interim period, I held an evangelistic campaign in Chalhuanca's Council auditorium. Eric Willett, a missionary from the other side of Apurímac, had joined me along with his wife and family. He brought Christian films that we projected as the central part of our evening presentations. Many attended the meetings and several young people accepted Christ. That was a motive for joy. Thereafter, I rushed back to Cuzco, being delayed by two landslides along the way. It was all worth it when I was present and witnessed the birth of our daughter, Rebecca Ann, on the 27th November 1975. Dot Patton was the midwife and Dr Nat Davies was somewhere near during the delivery. I was incredulous at how we had been so blessed.

From Cuzco, and when Rebecca was only six days old, we travelled by plane to Lima and on to Field Conference in Tarapoto, San Martín. It was great to meet all the RBMU field missionaries, and travelling within Peru became a pattern that continued during our time in Peru. This was not to augur well for church

---

4 He was the oldest living former Peruvian President at 97 years of age at the time of my writing this account.

planting. Indeed, rumblings of discontent at the Conference and ominous talk of separation of the UK and North American Boards did not encourage Jeannie and me in our "mixed marriage". Following Field Conference, Jeannie and I stayed on in Lima for me to study Quechua for three months in the Language School of Saint James Society. The course was intense and I suffered a migraine in class that led to temporary blindness and to me being hospitalised. Somehow, I had managed to get a bus home through the pain and double vision. Fortunately, Cherry Noble was present in Lima to help Jeannie and me cope.

On return to Chalhuanca I learned that a vehicle (a second-hand VW minibus) had been bought for us with money we had raised. All that remained was for me to sign the documents. At least that was what I thought. The story was long and convoluted and the crux of it was that three owners appeared. The first owner sold it to the second and then to the third and then to me. I need to interject a confession. I duly signed the documents and was encouraged by a colleague to include a "gratification" (a bribe) in the documents before I became the legal owner. I will return to that below. Before I move on, I remember that there was a shortage of petrol. Jeannie and I were travelling back to Chalhuanca from Abancay with some of our church folk when we stopped for a plate of soup. As we entered the restaurant, I joked with a truck driver that I had managed to rob some petrol, escape from the police, and so be able to travel. In reality, Stewart McIntosh had given me some. Anyway, as I was speaking, I noticed a burly police officer glowering at me over his glass of beer. After finishing our soup, we crossed the river in the minibus and I noticed the chain across the road, outside the small police commercial traffic control, preventing me from driving on. On entering the office, the same police officer greeted me with aggression. He was drunk. He demanded to know who I was and declared that the small radio receiver in his hand heard me declare that I had robbed petrol. He also asked what I had against the police. When I commented that he had been in the restaurant, his reaction encouraged me to suggest that it must have been someone like him. I knew the situation was delicate!

I was glad that he did not look at my documents as our Peruvian identity booklets and passports were again in Lima waiting for renewal. I had handed him my *"Libreta Tributaria"*, a Peruvian official document related to tax declarations and the control of money. At that time there were no governmental guarantees which meant he could, as he was threatening, lock me up, or do even worse. From the minibus, Jeannie heard all the shouting (the police officer's) and grew scared. Indeed, on discovering that I was Scottish, the officer told me that he would advise the Scottish Embassy about me! Nicola Sturgeon would have revelled in that possibility as prophetic. I prayed, and in my heart asked for the Lord to help. It was then that I simply said, "Thank you so much officer for how well you have treated me. If it were not so I would have to make an official complaint in Abancay." To this day I have seldom seen such a change in a man. The officer turned to me and said, "My name is [I cannot remember what it was], please do not ever repeat your behaviour", and he handed me my "documents". After this twenty-minute exchange, I thanked the Lord as I returned to the car and determined to be more circumspect in my speech. Are politeness and self-control (and bluff!) ever wrong? Indeed, that experience was paradigmatic of many others that Jeannie and I, and indeed the entire family, encountered on several occasions over the years at police and army controls!

For the initial period that I had the minibus, I used it extensively. The problems began when the first owner claimed the vehicle was his. What came to light was that he had "sold" the vehicle to the second "owner" and then the second to the third person with the understanding that each would complete outstanding hire purchase payments in Lima. No more payments were made. The vehicle was taken off my hands by the police and placed in the care of the Ministry of Transport. Days, weeks and months passed as I travelled backwards and forwards from Chalhuanca to Abancay. Time was lost. Finally, and I do not know how, the first owner agreed with me that if I paid what he owed in Lima he would sign the vehicle directly to me. I had no choice and no guarantees, but I thank the Lord he kept his word. As soon as it was mine, and for the second time, we took it to Lima, sold it, and bought a VW Beetle registration number JI 2466. How could I forget? I never gave another "gratification" during my time in Peru. I can only believe that the Lord showed his mercy in the final result.

Absences from Chalhuanca had occurred on several occasions in 1975 and this was to continue during all our time there. This was bad strategy and gave no continuity to a church planting ministry. It was hard work to follow up those who made decisions for Christ, to gather them back and to seek to disciple them. I made trips on foot to several villages and was accompanied by Amílcar Castañeda, the second son to Felicitas. I well remember being as hungry as I had ever been beyond a village called Sarayca, when we were offered lunch. I received a plate with only two fried eggs and some onion salad while Amílcar was given only one egg with his salad. I was tempted to leave it like that — I could have eaten ten eggs. I once had beaten my older brothers, Robert and Ivan, in a fried egg eating contest when I was seventeen years of age. Ivan ate eight, Robert eleven (one with a double yoke, which he claimed to equal two eggs!!) and I twelve. I still think I won! I admit I did not feel too well for a few days afterwards. Ah, to return to my story. I shared one of my two eggs with Amílcar. We had the strength to reach the next village and to share the Gospel with more people. So it was that we attempted to reach remote villages with the message of Christ.

During 1976, the short-term Project Timothy programme continued. Jeannie's 18-year-old sister Becky Yoder (later Becky Drummond) joined us from the USA as did Mary Sewell from Scotland (later Dr Packer), along with others. Stewart McIntosh and I drove them from Lima on what turned out to be a horrendous trip. Och! Jeannie was delighted to have Becky nearby and Rebecca met her aunt who did her fair share of babysitting. It was good to have them there and under Chris Papworth's overall leadership, an intense programme was developed and implemented. There is no doubt as to the value of such short-term ministry, but, because of the nature of the terrain in the Andes, much time was given to travel and, in our case, being away from Chalhuanca. After all, it is almost a sin not to travel to Cuzco and then on to see Machu Picchu, the Lost City of the Incas. Jeannie reminded me that, during their visit, we were so short of money that we had to borrow from Becky to put food on the table. We did pay her back!

In 1977 Jeannie, Rebecca and I went for the first time over to Talavera[5] (in the Province of Andahuaylas) in the rainy season (January to March) to teach in the Peruvian Evangelical Church Bible Institute. It looked as though I would not be able to participate as I was diagnosed with hepatitis and had to take to my bed because of the acute discomfort and pain. We certainly prayed, along with others in the Mission, and after just a few days in bed, I was on my feet again. Jeannie attended to my needs while sick and maintained then, and ever since, that the Lord had certainly healed me. I concur.

Robert and Joan Hamilton had begun training leaders in Talavera years before our involvement. There were many more churches in that region in need of leaders. Stewart McIntosh and Chris Papworth had also gone before us. This was a new experience and Jeannie, Rebecca and I slept on mattresses on the floor in one room and shared meals with the students, all male at that time. Shortly after completing our stint in Talavera in 1977, Jeannie was again expecting and she began to have complications. With that in mind, we drove the long journey to the clinic in Urcos, where Rebecca had been born, and with assurances from Dr Nat Davies, returned to Chalhuanca. Unfortunately, Jeannie miscarried days after our return. We were disappointed, Jeannie was shattered, and I well remember the pain as I saw the foetus, somewhat bigger than my thumb.

Without a doubt, we were on a journey that would later lead to other opportunities in the future and so we travelled to Talavera again in 1978 for the first three months of the year. By then the McIntoshes had moved to Lima and we shared our time there as teachers with Chris and Jackie Papworth in 1978. In my desire to give continuity to the work in Chalhuanca, I travelled there and back one weekend from Talavera. On return I was ill and was diagnosed with acute appendicitis. That was an experience that neither Jeannie nor I will ever forget. I was admitted to the state hospital in Andahuaylas while Jeannie rushed around buying everything; I mean everything that was needed for the operation. She even bought the razor blade needed for preparatory purposes. That reminds me that the soapy water used was cold, so cold. Once everything was ready, Cherry Noble, by then working in Andahuaylas, decided to be present during the operation. She was a qualified nurse and she came to our rescue again, and not for the last time.

---

5 Our colleague Stewart McIntosh often repeated that "there was only one place worse than Talavera: namely, Talavera in the rain!"

I remember that my feet were over the edge of the operating table. I am considered to be of average stature in the UK at five feet nine inches in height. I mentioned to the doctor that the table was short and he stated that it was "because the equipment was Japanese"!!! I also remember being asked to count to ten after they administered the anaesthetic. I reached ten and asked what I should do next. I was told to do so again. I remember counting to four, but Cherry told me later that I reached seven. She also told me afterwards that cotton wool had been stuck on to the point of my nose so they could see that I was still breathing. Further, she recounted that when they made the first cut, my body leapt so much that they administered more anaesthetic. They did the job, and although medics have disputed my claim, I had no more stomach problems afterwards. Is there such a thing as a grumbling appendix? Since that time, I have always been impressed with our NHS. In recent years this appreciation has increased.

Our time in Chalhuanca was coming to an end. It was time to move on. During our ministry in Chalhuanca we had built on what others had done, including Cherry and Jackie and the McIntoshes and, of course, Rosemary Flack, Jessie Norton and Maureen Hurd. We had baptised about twenty new believers in the river. The Lord, in his providence, later led Amílcar, my faithful companion, to San José, Costa Rica, where he married his Bolivian bride. They are still in ministry there. I believe there is a church in Chalhuanca but not the same denomination we worked with. Later, when in Lima, we met different *Chalhuanquinos* who were evangelical Christians. That encouraged us to believe our work had not been in vain. Is it ever, in the Lord?

6
First Furlough
1978-1979

*"Don't be impressed with your own wisdom.
Instead fear the Lord and turn away from evil."
Proverbs 3:6*

It was in late April 1978 that we had said our goodbyes to our friends and fellow Christians in Chalhuanca. There was a complex list of documents to process in Lima, further complicated because of our two nationalities and Rebecca's Peruvian birth and rights to be a citizen of three countries. Over the years we have been careful to renew documents and obtain requisite visas on time and in different venues. Jeannie was again expecting and it was timely that we enjoyed a better diet in Lima before we travelled on to the United States. In fact, we each gained over 14 pounds in weight during our brief time in Lima! Bacon and eggs were such a treat, as was fresh sliced bread. We arrived in Delaware on the 15th June and, besides enjoying the summer temperatures, we revelled in a huge family reunion.

As far as Jeannie's church affiliation was concerned, things had moved on in Delaware and Bishop John Mishler had started the quick-growing Cannon Mennonite church a few years previously. It was because Jeannie had had her hair cut during her first year in Peru that she forfeited financial support and would have been excommunicated by her home church. Instead, Bishop Mishler had informed her at that time of the consequence of her actions in the eyes of her church and had invited her to be a member of the new church. It was a bitter-sweet experience for Jeannie, although she continued then, and to this day, to have friends there. With all due respect to those Mennonites who insisted, at that time, on a woman not cutting her hair, Jeannie has been content to develop her own hairstyle. Rules have also been modified since in some Mennonite churches there.

Nothing really prepared us for the UK summer weather. We were met by my brother Martin and his wife Sue in London on the 11th July 1978, and by Chris and Jackie Papworth. After renewing acquaintances with friends, family and the Mission office in London, we landed in the cold of Aberdeen Airport, in transit, and were met by my sister and her husband Gordon. When we flew on to the airport in Orkney, to be met by my parents and my father's cousin Jimmick Scott, Rebecca was the one to suffer the cold most in her little summer dress. We remedied that at our earliest convenience.

I suppose that the culture shock suffered by Jeannie was acute. At that time silence reigned in the Kirkwall Baptist church before the service commenced on Sundays. Also, I had not remembered how quiet meal times were in my own home. Her main struggle was to understand the Orcadian take on the English language. Furthermore, Jeannie was now over seven months pregnant. The important thing was that Jeannie met the family and came to see the family farm where I had grown up, by then owned and managed by my brother Ivan and his wife Moira.

My sister Doreen had been busy on our behalf. Indeed, she and her husband Gordon had been in contact with people they knew in Aberdeen and the result was, by agreement of all concerned, that I would pastor Woodside Congregational Church in the city while on furlough. In exchange we lived free of charge in the Manse. It was humbling to be given practically all the furniture we needed as well as a cooker, freezer and fridge. I was not to be paid a stipend as such, but was faithfully given £25/month and preached once each Sunday. Membership was small and aging, and my duties included pastoral visitation and, sadly, one funeral during my time there.

We had already decided on staying in Aberdeen because I had been accepted to study in the University of Aberdeen as a non-graduating MA student. The idea was that I should study in the Department of Religious Studies, under the tutelage of Professor Andrew F Walls, be examined in papers (an equivalent of one year's senior honours' studies) and be adjudged to have reached a standard equivalent to Second Class Honours (Upper Division). As a result, I would then return to the University a year later (1980–81) and be admitted to study for the degree of Master of Letters in Religion in Primal Societies over twelve months. More of this later.

We spent what was to be a good and busy year in Aberdeen. My older brother Ivan loaned us a Hillman Avenger free of charge, the Kirkwall County Council paid my University fees, RBMU called on me to speak at conferences, we were allowed breaks to travel to Orkney and I enjoyed preaching through Paul's Epistle to the Galatians. Professor Walls was one of the most gracious Christians I had ever met, and he guided me into four main areas of study — the Nineteenth Century Missionary Movement, Christianity in Africa, New Religious Movements in Primal Societies and the Phenomenology of Religion. I was led into a new world as I was taught by Dr Adrian Hastings (a Roman Catholic priest who had chosen to live in "filial disobedience" and had married), by Dr James Thrower (a very gracious declared atheist) and by Professor Walls who, besides being an academic and a Methodist by denominational affiliation, had been a missionary University lecturer in Sierra Leone, and shone as a people-person who had a great love for all things African. The majority of post-graduate students were African.

Of course, all of this was going on as we sought to register in the NHS. After initial paperwork and deliberation, Jeannie was duly enrolled and assigned to a very prestigious and small clinic. It gave us great joy when Samuel David Scott was born on the 7th September just as I was about to begin my studies. Jeannie and I worked out a system whereby I would walk the floor with Samuel until he settled in the evening and she would wake to feed him during the night. The Manse was cold so I prepared a kettle beside the bed within reach so I could prepare our morning cuppa in bed at the press of a button, get up, have breakfast and leave for classes while Jeannie recovered from the night in bed. It was great to have Gordon and Doreen nearby and their son Brendan, who became a playmate to Rebecca.

During the year so many people visited us, and I also invited students home for meals. I think most of them were living frugally, at least judging by the way they appreciated their food. Jeannie's younger sisters, Karen and Becky, came from the USA along with Jeannie's nephew Ronnie. We renewed fellowship with Mary Sewell, by then a medical student, and her boyfriend Alan Packer. We remain friends of the Packers to this day.

7
Andahuaylas, Apurímac
1979–1980

"Those who trust in me will never be put to shame."
Isaiah 49:23d

Jeannie, Rebecca and Samuel left Scotland for the United States on the 9th May 1979, while I stayed on with my sister Doreen and her husband Gordon, in order to study and to write a diet of three hour examinations in the university as well as speak in the Scottish RBMU Conference in Largs, near Glasgow. I joined my family in the USA on the 28th May and we then travelled on to Peru on the 8th June 1979. We had been allocated to work for a year in Andahuaylas, where Cherry Noble had moved to minister after Chris Papworth and Jackie Howe were married. Cherry selflessly allowed us to take possession of the house she rented while she found other accommodation in the town.

It was during the year in Andahuaylas that I, along with a new acquaintance Jacob Huamán Ccoicca and others, formed the Sociedad Misionera Evangélica de Apurímac (SOMEA—translatable as the Evangelical Missionary Society of Apurímac). The idea grew in me that the best way to evangelise the other side of Apurímac was by sending Peruvians from Andahuaylas with Peruvian money. Indeed, by this stage I had become convinced that the best church planters were not foreign missionaries but Peruvians. This was not an absolute conclusion as missionaries such as Fred Webb (in RBMU in San Martín and Amazonas) and Robert Hamilton (with the Andes Evangelical Mission in Andahuaylas and later in other missions in Lima and Chile) and others were notable exceptions. Nevertheless, I believed then, and still do to this day, that nationals are more effective church planters than foreign missionaries.

Jeannie and I were struck by the fact that there were numerous churches in the Province of Andahuaylas, whereas on the other side, such as in the provinces of Chalhuanca, Antabamba, Grau and Abancay, there were few. Of course, the Evangelical Union of South America had placed missionaries in Andahuaylas decades before RBMU's involvement. However, this was also so in Abancay and the Tysons had ministered there, but with limited success. Without going into the history of the Peruvian Evangelical Church in Apurímac, what became evident was that church growth occurred, more often than not, because entire families came to Christ. More families were then persuaded to turn to Christ by others who lived in the villages. The human element was certainly present, but more importantly the divine element was, and is, crucial. On a personal level as

I had gone from village to village, either alone or with others, many had made "decisions" to follow Christ. Of course, in Chalhuanca I had neither the infrastructure, the time, nor the wherewithal to return and disciple them. Indeed, most of those who attended our church there were young people. I noted that where I was asked by a family, before preaching, to make an invitation, those people continued in the newfound faith. It was because they had already made their decision to follow Christ before the meeting. What happened at the end of the meeting should not really be attributed to the sermon but to what God had already done through His instruments, that is, the local Christians. There were practically no cultural barriers or misunderstandings as families won families. God was at work in his way and to Him be the glory.

The year in Andahuaylas was important for us; Jeannie and I made some lasting Peruvian friends, we met believers from the numerous churches on that side of Apurímac and I had met Jacob Huamán Ccoicca, who not only became a friend but, on our return to Abancay in late 1981, would become a pioneer in a new outreach. At the risk of getting ahead of myself, I think it appropriate to mention that SOMEA, mentioned above, continues today (February 2019) and since the 1980s, scores of churches have been planted. Indeed, not only have churches in Andahuaylas supported the outreach financially but also with personnel. On any given Sunday, members of the Abancay church will travel for several hours on a truck, get off, walk to remote villages, present Christ, and then make the long journey back to Abancay. Those involved can tell stories that smack of the action of the Holy Spirit in the New Testament. There is no doubt in my mind that the Lord is building his Church with, and mostly without, foreign missionaries.

Our "year" in Andahuaylas was cut short because Jeannie fell ill with hepatitis and had to take to bed. It was a difficult time and we had to employ some help, who often carried Samuel around on her back while cooking and cleaning. I was teaching in the Talavera Bible Institute. Indeed, I had to travel to Lima for some meetings and drove to Ayacucho along with Rebecca, staying overnight in the Rev Robert Woodson's (Presbyterian missionary) home before Rebecca and I took the plane on to Lima. I remember we stayed in the RBMU Mission flat in Miraflores in Lima, where Fred and Ruth Webb (RBMU missionaries) accompanied us.

On return to Andahuaylas it seemed that Jeannie had not improved substantially, so we made the decision, along with field leadership, to travel to Lima earlier than planned. Jeannie, Rebecca and Samuel flew down from Andahuaylas and were looked after by Stewart and Janet McIntosh in Lima until my arrival by road. I remember driving down to Lima in our blue VW Beetle in the company of Cherry's landlord, Ramón Echegaray. He and I took turns to drive and arrived at the Mcintosh's at some unearthly hour of the early morning. Although Jeannie was slowly on the mend, months passed after our return home to Scotland before she was well.

8
Second Furlough
1980–1981

*"Don't love money; be satisfied with what you have.
For God has said, 'I will never fail you. I will never abandon you.'"*
Hebrews 13:5

Our desire was to return to Abancay in Apurímac after furlough and initiate SOMEA as a viable means of planting churches. Before that became possible, we travelled to the USA on the 9th June 1980. During our time there, I worked on teams building huge chicken houses for Sam Yoder and Sons, a company owned by Jeannie's oldest brother. It was good to be again with Jeannie's extended family, for me to be able to earn some much-needed money and for us all to be prepared for the next step. To be honest, I thought the work in temperatures of up to 40 degrees would kill me. After the first day I could hardly walk, during the second day I thought I was going to die for sure, and when it came to the third day, I "knew" I was going to die. After that it got easier and I learned new skills. It was a blessing to be among Mennonites and I was asked to preach in different Mennonite churches. I was careful to dress appropriately, i.e. without a tie, without Jeannie (on occasion) and without my wedding ring, when so required.

Before we arrived back in the UK on the 5th August 1980, my ever-enterprising sister Doreen had scouted for accommodation for us. She found a cottage near Banchory, some twenty miles from Aberdeen, called Little Minklets. What a great name! It was arranged with the Adams family that, in exchange for six hours of farm labour per week at Bush Farm, we could have the place rent free. The cottage was small and we set about furnishing it at minimal cost. It was not unlike Peru, as it was a case of who "we knew", or rather in this case, who Gordon and Doreen knew. My brother Ivan extended the loan of the same Hillman Avenger as before. We had agreed with RBMU that we would receive no support from the Mission during furlough, until completion of studies in the University of Aberdeen and arrival back in Peru.

The year in Little Minklets became one of the most enjoyable years of our lives. Rebecca started into Primary One in Crathes Primary School, less than a mile away. Samuel was in his element watching "Charlie Adam's tractor" as it went past. Jeannie returned to full health. We had more visitors, including family from the USA, my parents from Orkney, and friends and family from all over the UK. I was able to work on the farm, making hay and silage, until classes began in October and thus earn some money. I was careful to keep meticulous accounts over the duration of the entire year and recorded that we had an income averaging £70/week from all sources—including money sent to us by supporters—and of that an average of £20/week were spent on petrol and the car. Furthermore, as on our previous visit to Aberdeen, we ended the year debt free. This time I paid my own fees in the University. Jeannie certainly proved herself as a master of eking out a budget. Baked potatoes prepared in the embers of the oven-fire in the living room were our favourite. Jeannie knew how to add on trimmings. Our Asda shop every two weeks included every offer they had and averaged £30 bi-weekly.

Indeed, with hindsight, the year was an oasis to us at every level before our return to Peru. The above paragraph is a testimony to the Lord's faithfulness. Jeannie and I do not doubt that the Lord had prepared us for the year through previous experiences. My farm upbringing came back to me and recent building experience in the USA led to new abilities that helped me adapt to farm work again. The winter months would see me scramble out of bed in the cold—there was no heating in the bedroom—to feed cattle, have devotions and breakfast and then drive the 20 miles to university for classes. I loved my studies and while back in the cottage, would don my overcoat, scarf and gloves to pass hours in study in our cold bedroom.

The academic study of the following three subjects was enjoyable: World Views of Primal Societies, Archaic Religions and their Penetration of Primal Societies and New Religious Movements in Primal Societies. After successfully passing my diet of examinations, we took a break in Orkney and then I turned my attention to the dissertation. I had begun investigating a Peruvian New Religious Movement in 1978 and intensified that research in 1979–80. I was awarded the MLitt degree in December 1981.

My university studies taught me how to study another religion, not from a standpoint of what I think might be believed, but from "within", by paying attention to what believers in that religion would "tell me they believed". I learned to "suspend judgement" while carrying out the investigation, and how to "place into parenthesis my own faith" until such a time as I might be able to draw conclusions. I believe this has enabled me, without moving from my own convictions, to show more empathy and respect towards those who do not believe as I do. I am still learning to extend this respect, not only to all other Christians, but to those of other faiths and those who profess none.

9
Abancay, Apurímac
1981–1984

> "But go to Him when your need is desperate,
> when all other help is vain,
> and what do you find?
> A door slammed in your face,
> and a sound of bolting on the inside.
> After that, silence."
> C. S. Lewis in *A Grief Observed*.

When we all returned to Peru on the 20th October 1981, via the USA, I had been asked to teach in November at post-graduate level in the Department of Missiology in the Lima Evangelical Seminary. Stewart McIntosh and Tito Paredes were instrumental in that invitation and this marked a new commitment to the Department of Missiology within the Seminary. My assigned area was that of New Religious Movements in Primal Societies and I majored on the Israelites of the New Universal Covenant, a new Peruvian religious group, and the subject of my recent university dissertation. It was also to become the focus of my PhD several years later.

It was after our return in late 1981 that we sold our VW Beetle and purchased a Suzuki jeep along with the recently arrived Dutch couple Louis and Ellen Sterkenburg and their small new-born son Gedeon. The Sterkenburgs had arrived fresh from language studies in Costa Rica and they were to share both the vehicle and ministry with us in Abancay. Before then several things happened. I was elected to be RBMU field leader at our conference in December 1981. It was a personal choice for me to change the nomenclature from that of Field Director to that of Field Coordinator. It seemed more appropriate to me as I considered myself as one among equals. Indeed, who was I to "direct" colleagues who had much more experience in ministry than I did?

Soon afterwards, Jeannie, Rebecca, Samuel and I travelled by road in the Suzuki to Apurímac. The journey was to prove momentous. Although the jeep was new, it gave us some problems in Lima. We thought that the issue had been rectified, but as we left sea level in Nazca, some 300 miles from the capital, and climbed into the altitude, it was obvious that something was wrong. Further along the journey we were forced to stay the night in a hotel in Puquio. It was so cold that Jeannie shared her bed with Rebecca and I mine with Samuel. We piled on the layers of blankets. Early the next day, after taking the vehicle to a mechanic, who assured us all was now well, we set off again. It was soon clear that all was not well because we made sporadic progress across many miles of rough roads. The car finally stopped and would not start. We estimated that we were pretty much at the highest part of the journey. It was cold, a drunken "fiesta" was happening not too far from the road and we heard insults directed towards us *gringos*. It would not have been safe to stay the night in such an isolated place and the cold would soon have set in.

Our only option was prayer, although this was not the first time we had prayed during the journey. By this stage we had no option but to pray with total dependency on the Lord. We focussed and asked the Lord to "rescue" us from the predicament. It was then that I felt constrained to get out of the car and release a bolt to allow petrol to run out of the carburettor. I had/have practically no mechanical knowledge, although I did know that petrol passed through there. I will leave any other attempt at explanation. After securing the bolt I returned to my seat and turned the ignition key. The Suzuki sprang into life and took us without a further splutter to Chalhuanca before it decided to stop! Maybe we needed that to believe that what had happened was indeed a class "A" miracle. With God there are no class "B" miracles. We stayed the night in a hotel, had the carburettor looked at again the next day, and journeyed on, to arrive at Cherry Noble's house in Andahuaylas late in the afternoon.

The Sterkenburgs flew up to Andahuaylas some weeks afterwards when they had obtained their Peruvian documents. I remember that Cherry accommodated us all somewhere. We were in Andahuaylas with a view to finding suitable housing to rent in Abancay and the wait and uncertainty were a challenge to our patience. Both Louis and I made it a priority to find two places in Abancay and we travelled there several times in our search. Indeed, before our final move over there, I distinctly remember that little Gedeon had developed one of the angriest and most painful nappy rashes I had ever witnessed.

What did I know? The doctors were not able to prescribe any suitable cure. I will never forget that I was carrying Gedeon outside the house one evening in order to give Louis and Ellen a break and I was asking the Lord to "heal" the wee fellow. It was then that the word "foam rubber" came to me. I went in and asked if Gedeon was sleeping on a foam rubber mattress. The answer was affirmative and after suggesting placing him on something else, he began to get better immediately. Any doubts about the Lord's intervention were removed when, a few days later, the wee fellow managed to pick some foam rubber from a mattress and rub it on his face. He came out in red welts immediately.

Other realities that cannot be overlooked were all the changes that had occurred on the socio-political front during our absence and on into our final time in Abancay, Apurímac. Fernando Belaúnde Terry, as the 57th President of Peru, had been deposed by a military coup in 1968. What had followed were twelve years of military rule. Belaúnde was democratically re-elected as the 60th President of Peru in 1980. During his second presidency (28th July 1980–28th July 1985) he was again recognised for his personal integrity and for his commitment to the democratic process. One of the first actions after his inauguration was that he gave back freedom of speech by returning newspapers to their rightful owners.

Nevertheless, and in spite of a promising beginning, his popularity began to be eroded by rising inflation, economic hardships, the decline in per capita income, the burgeoning foreign debt and the rise of violence by leftist insurgents, notably the Shining Path. Terrorism grew steadily during the internal conflict in Peru to the extent that a state of emergency was declared in the Ayacucho and Apurímac regions. During the Falklands War in 1982, President Belaúnde would declare himself ready to support Argentina with the resources that it needed. *El Niño* affected Peru adversely in 1982 and 1983 through widespread flooding, severe droughts and reduced schools of fish from the ocean. Fish was one of the country's major resources.

I believe it true to state that we were not unaffected by the above changes and it is timely to record Jeannie's input to life at grass roots level:

> *In February 1982 we moved to Abancay, the capital of the department of Apurímac. It was not as high an altitude as either Chalhuanca or Andahuaylas, which meant that it had a more temperate climate. This had both advantages and disadvantages. It meant that we did not need as much warm clothing and we had warm sunshine most days. The not-so-pleasant aspects of its climate were the little vicious flies that could bite in a nanosecond and leave itchy welts. They especially liked ankles and elbows! We also had tarantulas that appeared, and I became quite good at making them disappear with the flat side of a straw broom. One day I was washing Rebecca's hair at the outside sink when we both noticed a tarantula's legs poking up through the drain. Fortunately, there was a cover over the drain, but we made quick work of the hair-washing that day. Every night when the children went to bed, I checked the walls, the floors and even under the bedclothes to make sure there were no scorpions around. I don't think they had a deadly sting, but it could be unpleasant, so we took every precaution.*
>
> *Because Rebecca had started school in Scotland while we were on furlough, I decided to home school her and Sam, when he was ready for Primary 1. We had made arrangements with an English educational provider to send us all the materials we might need and I, in turn, would report to them with samples of Rebecca's work, to be marked and evaluated. We made one of the rooms in our house "the school room", where we spent mornings doing our schoolwork.*
>
> *Ken continued to travel frequently, and with his added responsibility as Mission Coordinator, he was often away either travelling to villages or to Lima for meetings. He and I had no means of communication in those days, and with two children to look after, I was often aware of the Lord's protection and help. I was so thankful that Ken was at home when Rebecca became quite unwell and broke out in red blotches over her legs. The doctor came and had a look but stated that he had no idea what it was. He went away but returned the next day*

> to tell us that he had looked through his medical books until he found out what it was. I cannot remember the name he gave it, but he was able to treat it and Rebecca was soon well again.
>
> During one of Ken's trips away, I got sick and felt like it might be my time to go. The Sterkenburgs, who worked with us in Abancay, sent a doctor to see if he knew what the problem was. He immediately diagnosed typhoid fever. Louis and Ellen took Rebecca and Sam to their house and left me on my own! I guess they thought they were taking the children out of harm's way! They dropped off a flask of broth at my front door each day, which was welcome. They also got the medicine that had been prescribed. When Ken returned from his trip, I greeted him with, "Don't kiss me, I have typhoid fever!" He soon brought the children home, and it wasn't too long before I was on my feet again.
>
> We enjoyed our time in Abancay. We had space to have a small garden, grow flowers and have both chickens and rabbits.

Whereas Louis and Ellen were settling into life in Abancay in early 1982, I was to be involved again in teaching in the Bible Institute in Talavera. I would like to relate some experiences shared along with a team of students from the institute. Each year included outreach by the students to remote villages in Apurímac. In order to link in with what Jeannie wrote above, I believe it not inappropriate to tell of this one specific trip. Indeed, this one experience could be representative of many others in the subsequent years.

Louis drove me to Andahuaylas on Wednesday the 17th February 1982 and returned to Abancay. The next day, I travelled in a truck with a mixed team of eight students (Cherry had rightly encouraged the inclusion of female students), to a place called Huancaray. The rains were too heavy for us to move on, so we stayed the night and believers there gave us accommodation. On Friday the 19th we travelled to San Antonio de Cachi in another truck. On arrival we received a message from Chulisana, our intended final destination, that it might not be convenient to join them. I decided to ask Jacob Huamán Ccoicca, along with Esther and María (both from the region) to walk to Chulisana as a forward envoy in order to find out if we could join them. The rest of us stayed on where we were and shared Bible studies with the believers in their homes. On Sunday we met with the few believers from the village for worship. Indeed, we almost outnumbered them.

The Christians in San Antonio de Cachi shared their soup, guinea pigs, boiled maize, potatoes, eggs, milk and avocados with us. I wrote the following in my journal before turning in on Sunday evening the 21st of February 1982:

> It has been raining and during the day we have each shared different meditations from Scripture with our brothers and sisters in Christ. The Lord blessed us all together. I really am missing Jeannie and the kids. It does not get any easier to be apart, but I am glad I came. Nevertheless, I hope to be able to omit such long absences from home in the future—14 days represents a long time.

The next day (Monday the 22nd February) I recorded the following:

> In the morning we had a prayer meeting at which I spoke briefly on Jonah chapter 4. After breakfast at Gumercindo's house—guinea pig, boiled potatoes, bread and *mate* [herbal tea]—we were invited to María's parents' house where we were served corn soup. I could not finish mine—just too much food. We left on foot for Chulisana at 9.50am. We were met on the way by a brother from there and, when we arrived at the river, by Jacob and María. By that stage I was worried about the steep climb on the way back…
>
> The rains had caused the river to damage the bridge. Some workmen at the river wanted donations so they could buy more *trago* [alcohol]. I was careful to shake each man's hand and then we tackled the very steep climb to Chulisana. At one stage Jacob helped me with my backpack. After arrival in the village we had lunch in Francisco Elías Gonzales' house. We were each served two plates of soup—an acceptable food for me always…
>
> After lunch we all went out to see the *Fiesta (Carnavál)* but drunks kept bothering me, so I tried to stay indoors. One can surely see the difference between believers and unbelievers. It was going to be difficult to share Christ during such festivities…
>
> The believers up here really suffer persecution and have done for years. Their faith costs them and I find it a privilege to share with them…

It was proving to be a difficult week and I had sent part of our team to another village called Ccapcca where there were more believers. The plan was for them to return to us on Friday the 26th with believers from that village, and for us to have a day of fasting and prayer and to celebrate the Lord's Supper together. I was taking a stroll outside on Wednesday, along with Juan and María, when I became aware, through my limited Quechua, that several men were coming in our direction. María advised me quietly to return to the house. One of the leaders (*el agente*) held a whip and challenged me to a fight. I confess, to my shame, that for a moment I was tempted to take him out but thought better of it and started walking slowly towards the house. He raised his whip behind me and was insulting me as a coward. It was then that María placed herself behind me and he desisted from any more than continuing to shout insults.

In light of what was happening, I sent Jacob, Gregorio, María and Esther to Ccapcca so that they could encourage the believers there. Indeed, those who lived there had also been insulted by those who lived in Chulisana. I noted in my diary that I was using some time to read and prepare studies in the book of Revelation for my classes in March. The *Fiesta* continued all night outside. We had our usual meetings on the inside and were careful not to be in the patio, to avoid the falling stones that were being thrown indiscriminately at us. Thursday was spent in fasting. I was glad of a break from food. We only had herbal tea to drink and interspersed the day with Bible studies and prayer.

It was on Friday the 26th that we discovered the town was set on "denouncing" us in the nearest police station in San Antonio de Cachi. Apparently, we were to be accused of attempting to burn down the Catholic Church during the night, that one of the male students had hit the *agente* (a veiled reference to the episode above), and that two of the students had made out in the maize field outside the village. After making sure that none of the above was true, and after celebrating the Lord's Supper, together with a group from Ccapcca, I decided it was time to act.

Our host, Francisco, accompanied me to see the *Juez* (Judge) in the village. In such remote places, local people were normally elected to be authorities. That particular "judge" told me, after some cold formalities and introductions, that he only had a Primary School education. He used this to remonstrate with me that, as an educated man, I should know better than allow my team to act as they had been accused. I remember that he and I discussed the impartiality of any judge. I also remember his response, that whereas his office required him to be impartial, he could not be so when it came to the religion of his village. He railed against Francisco and the "false" religion of us "evangélicos". Therefore, he asked me to be present at the General Assembly of the village in the central square on Sunday the 28th when the accusations would be made. It was, he declared, for his village to make a judgement on us.

I had to make a wise choice. On the one hand I knew that the Peruvian constitution upheld freedom of religion, and I had failed in my attempt to present that case to the judge. On the other hand, because of the rise of insurgency, I knew that a state of emergency had been declared in Ayacucho and Apurímac. What tipped the balance was that, during the evening, a well-wisher came to warn us that select villagers had been asked by their leaders to make sure they had enough stones gathered to attack the "gringo" and the others on Sunday. He advised us that we should leave and thus avoid the danger of violence.

Two brothers from the group accompanied Gregorio and me as we left for San Antonio de Cachi early on Saturday the 27th. It was a little uncanny to see and hear doors open as we walked out of Chulisana. No one in any doorway responded to my greetings of "buenos días"! After a strenuous (for me—not them) three hour walk we duly went to the small police station in San Antonio de Cachi and presented our official complaint. My companions enabled me to include names and to list the full extent of unlawful behaviour committed against us during our stay in Chulisana. The police duly sent a notice to those named and asked them to appear. They never did respond. In fact, and unknown to us at the time, the authorities from Chulisana had sent a delegation, during the previous night, all the way to Huancaray and on to the Sub Prefect in Andahuaylas to lodge their (false) accusations.

Before being joined by the others from Ccapcca and Chulisana that same day, Gregorio and I had our first real body-wash in over a week. We stayed over the weekend in San Antonio de Cachi, sharing fellowship again in a friendly atmosphere, and then travelled over two days to Andahuaylas. I was looking forward to seeing Jeannie, Rebecca and Sam when I got off the truck in Abancay on March the 4th and walked several streets to our front door. I did not expect Jeannie's greeting: "Don't kiss me, I have typhoid fever." I was back and went as quickly as I could to bring Rebecca and Samuel home. My priority was to nurse Jeannie back to health.

The next few months were not any easier. I suffered a car accident when I struck a small girl who ran in front of the Suzuki in Abancay. I took both parents and the child to the hospital. Fortunately, the wee girl was not severely injured, although the parents made all kinds of threats, asked for money and even accused me of stealing her x-rays from the hospital! It felt as if I was on a lonely journey. I remember reading Scripture and James 1:2 challenged me: "Dear brothers and sisters, when troubles come your way, consider it an opportunity for great joy". The "official" investigation of what happened in Chulisana dragged on. Jeannie was not well. I confess that I came to the point in my morning devotions to say to the Lord, "Please Lord, no more!"

It was that day that the parents of the little girl agreed to sign a legally binding document before a Public Notary that they would not ask any more of me. The Chulisana event ended in no more than a severe reprimand from the Sub-Prefect for us all. By that time, it was too late for the leaders of that village, as Shining Path guerrillas arrived a few weeks after we had been there. They gathered the population in the central square and demanded to know whether their leaders were just or unjust. When, in unison, those present answered negatively, the leaders were summarily executed. That still brings a shiver to my spine. Nevertheless, from that time, the local church in Chulisana began to grow.

The pattern had been set and I was often away from home for weeks at a time. It was great that Louis and Ellen dedicated themselves to give continuity to ministry in the Abancay church, although Louis did accompany Jacob and me on trips to different Provinces in Apurímac. Jacob came to Abancay as one of the first missionaries of SOMEA. He lived with the Sterkenburgs. Two others had also joined SOMEA from the Andahuaylas side and were placed in Chalhuanca. They left, without telling anyone, when they discovered the possibility of prospecting for gold in the Jungle! I made several trips, along with Jacob, looking everywhere to find them, until the news filtered through regarding their whereabouts. Lessons were to be learned. At one stage during the Falklands War (2nd April–14th June 1982), we decided to gather all RBMU UK citizens in Lima, just in case we would be asked to leave Peru. There are stories to tell, but not here.

Insurgency was on the increase and all missionaries in Apurímac testified to difficult experiences, especially when travelling. Sadly, reports of killings increased, and many Christians lost their lives when they would not deny their faith. Others were falsely imprisoned by the security forces. Both the insurgents and the military did their worst. I wish I could add that I had ceased to travel as much. I remember in 1983 returning home with Jacob, for three days, from a fruitful trip to the Province of Grau. I also remember Jeannie's reaction when I informed her that, as Field Co-ordinator, I was due to travel again, this time to Amazonas in the North of Peru. She replied: "Just go!" During my two weeks I had plenty of time to reflect. I calculated that I was seated on a bus for eight days altogether. The good news about that trip was that I travelled, along with a leader of the Peruvian Evangelical Church (Saúl Barrera) so that 17 churches, planted by RBMU missionaries Fred and Ruth Webb, May Walker, Elaine Webster and David and Helena Stevens, could join the Peruvian denomination.

Although I could have recorded numbers of "decisions" for Christ on different occasions, that would be misleading. I had become aware that the biblical command in Matthew 28 was to "make disciples". The Scriptures teach that the "seed" of God's Word falls on soil but not all soils produce fruit. Also, the "wheat and the tares" grow together and may look the same, but they are not. Incidentally, I had reason to conclude that danger and persecution had a way of throwing up clues as to true spiritual identity, although it is not my calling to judge what will not be finally clear until reaching glory. Forgive me for stating that the easy task was to ask for people to make decisions.

The costly ministry of making disciples was taking time and perseverance. However, that is precisely where we found evidence of Jesus' promise to build His Church. People were "being added to the Church". When we left Abancay, a new group of believers had come to faith above the city. Jacob was certainly instrumental in that development and he had also met the lady there who was to become his wife.

By early 1984 we had reached the sad decision, with Mission approval, that our time in Abancay was coming to an end. With that in view, after teaching once more in the Bible Institute in Talavera, we travelled to Lima in late April in order to teach in the Lima Seminary and to renew our Peruvian visas and travel documents. We all (Jeannie, Rebecca, Samuel and I) left Abancay on a bus bound for Cuzco and for our onward flight to Lima. A lasting memory was that Jacob had waited on the road above the city, along with some new believers, to wave a final goodbye as we passed by.

Jacob Huamán developed into a leader in Apurímac and he became both the President of the Synod of the Apurímac Peruvian Evangelical Church and Director of the Bible Institute in Talavera. He wrote to me recently (February 2019) and included details of over 50 churches planted in three Provinces in Apurímac during the decades since our departure, both through SOMEA and local church activities. Pastor Luís Hernán Cervantes in Abancay was but a boy back then and the Lord has blessed his ministry there as a burgeoning missionary church developed. José Feliciano Sánchez, from Andahuaylas, told stories of miracles and mass conversions in the midst of persecution and violence in the 1980s. Our contribution was tiny in contrast to theirs. Above all, and without any doubt, the Lord merits glory.

10
Third Furlough
1984–1985

*"So we can say with confidence,
'The Lord is my helper, so I will have no fear.
What can mere people do to me?'"
Hebrews 13:6*

Soon after arrival in the United States on the 28th July 1984, we moved into Jeannie's step-father's caravan on his farm in Greenwood, Delaware. Jeannie's brother Doyle and his wife Mary-Jane were neighbours. Rebecca and Samuel were enrolled in the Greenwood Mennonite School. They enjoyed their studies and discovered cousins and other more-distant relatives! I went through the pain barrier again as I worked for Sam Yoder and Sons. We were glad of the income. The UK pound had fallen to $1.05/£ and our mission allowance would not have been enough. I severed a tendon on my right hand when unloading roofing steel and was unable to continue for several weeks. Although I had preached in several Mennonite churches there on different visits, I had never been remunerated before. It all changed and I was also "paid" for speaking at the spiritual emphasis week in the Mennonite School. We received almost exactly the amount I would have earned during the same period of work.

When we entered the UK through Heathrow Airport on the 7th November 1984, Jeannie was only granted a visa for four months. We had already chosen to spend our furlough in Orkney. My brother Ivan and his wife Moira kindly offered us one of the farm cottages to live in. It gave me a sense of nostalgia to be back on the family farm and it was just fine to be near my folks. Rebecca and Samuel were enrolled in the Dounby School, next to where I had pastored when all-too-young. Our children travelled to school along with two of Ivan and Moira's four children, their cousins Sharon and Jonathon. It was a harsh winter, which pleased the children when they were given time off school. I accompanied another RBMU missionary (John Wilson—missionary in Irian Jaya) on a Scottish University tour (Aberdeen[6], Dundee, Edinburgh and Glasgow) and besides being glad of the company, I enjoyed the interaction with university students.

---

[6] While passing through Aberdeen in January 1985 I took the opportunity to enrol for a PhD.

The highlight for me was a separate deputation trip to Stornoway on the isle of Lewis. As a boy I had remembered Duncan Campbell share in the Kirkwall Baptist Church regarding "the mighty movement of God" on the island in 1949. On my deputation trip I preached in a Church of Scotland on Sunday morning and in a large gathering in a hall in the evening. Two memories stayed with me. Firstly, I recall that Duncan Campbell believed that two old ladies brought the revival through their prayers. A Presbyterian minister who knew them told me they were shocked by this. They declared: "How dare he suggest that. The Lord did it all!" Secondly, while at an after-meeting fraternal on Sunday evening, the folk I was staying with indicated one of the elderly minister's wives who was saved in the revival, who from that time, when she prayed, often "went off in what seemed like another language". They asked me: "What do you make of that?"

11
Lima
1985–1987

"The depravity of man is at once the most empirically verifiable reality but at the same time the most intellectually resisted fact."
Malcolm Muggeridge

Alan García Pérez served as President of Peru from 1985 to 1990 and again from 2006 to 2011 to be the 61st and 64th President of Peru respectively. His first term was marked by a severe economic crisis, social unrest and violence. Insurgency was on the increase in the Andes and in Lima. During the 1980s tens of thousands died, including, according to some conservative estimates, over 500 evangelical church leaders. The Sterkenburgs moved to Cuzco two years after our exit from Apurímac as the situation became too dangerous for them. Many stories emerged from that period of the Lord's miraculous delivery of some Christians but also of the martyrdom of others. Those stories are not my stories or I would include them here. Numerous evangelical churches trace their origins and growth to that period.

We arrived back from Scotland in Lima on the 3rd March 1985 and immediately began our search for accommodation. We moved initially into a large colonial-styled house in the San Isidro district of Lima, at a very modest rent. We certainly had enough space. Our move to Peru's capital was, in part, designed to accommodate the children's education and to investigate possibilities for me of a wider teaching ministry. I became part of the Department of Missiology in the Lima Evangelical Seminary on a part-time basis and was able to teach my speciality-subject on New Religious Movements as one of the required post-graduate subjects. Once students had completed course prerequisites, it was a new experience for me to be assigned to supervise several dissertations: the final part of their postgraduate *Licenciatura en Misiología* degree. Rubén Zavala was one of my students who not only completed his dissertation on a history of the Assemblies of God in Lima in 1987, but then published that history in 1989. Besides this, I did some teaching in the Peruvian Evangelical Church's Night Bible Institute, preached in both my local church as well as in others, and spoke in several conferences.

Before long I was voted in again as the RBMU Field Co-ordinator and that involved me in a certain amount of administration and pastoral visitation of missionaries. On one such visit to Apurímac, two French tourists were shot dead by a fifteen year old female "terrorist" just a few miles away from where I stayed with colleagues.

Life took on a more regular routine in Lima than when we lived in the Andes and I travelled less away from home. Jeannie developed her own role outside of the home and that contributed to the shape of our lives in Lima. Her input on the Lima "experience" outlines that period of our lives:

> *When we moved to Lima in 1985, we enrolled Rebecca and Samuel in a Peruvian School called "María Alvarado", previously known as Lima High School. It was established by American Methodists to train girls in secretarial skills and English. A few years before we arrived in Lima, after the military takeover in 1968, the school had been mandated to change its name. Soon afterwards it opened enrolment to boys and broadened its education curriculum.*
>
> *The school years in Peru run from April to December and not long into the academic year I received a phone call asking me if I would be interested in teaching in the same school. I was a qualified teacher, but, apart from home schooling the children, I hadn't been in a classroom for a long time. I agreed to give it a go and was assigned to teach English to the equivalent of third and fourth year secondary students, during five days each week.*
>
> *However, I was not prepared for the shock of distinguishing names and faces — all the same skin colour, same eye colour, same hair colour and same uniform colour! Somehow, I did eventually find differences that made the students individuals, and I found that I enjoyed helping them with their spoken English, grammar and composition.*
>
> *Living in Lima was different for me in other ways, too. I was interacting with women I could communicate with in Spanish and I was not quite such a foreigner in Lima as I had been in the Andes.*
>
> *We attended a small church not far from our home and after a few months there, I began to teach a ladies' Bible class on Sunday mornings. One memory of that class stands out: in Spanish every believer gets the title of "brother" or "sister". Quite often the person's Christian name is not included. This means that potentially, one could attend a fellowship without ever knowing anyone's Christian name. I determined in my ladies' class that it would be different, and I insisted on calling each lady by her Christian name as well as "sister"; i.e. Sister Miriam, Sister Ruth, and expected them to do the same. I will never know if they continued to do so after I left.*
>
> *Because Ken was co-ordinator of our mission during our years in Lima, we were responsible for organising prayer times and fellowship meals for us all. Our colleagues became family, not only for us, but for our children as well.*

In early 1986 we received the news that Jeannie's mum had taken seriously ill with cancer and was not expected to live. We decided that Jeannie and Rebecca should travel to the USA for a visit. In the meantime, Samuel and I travelled to Andahuaylas for me to teach in the Bible Institute in Talavera. Meg Swanson (now Mrs Morgan), a single lady missionary from Thurso, Scotland, made sure we were well-catered for and that Samuel got into a minimum of mischief while I was teaching.

During those years in Lima (1985–1986) I had been doing research with a view to writing my PhD thesis on return to Scotland. In 1987 I intensified my visits to both the administrative offices and religious meetings of a Peruvian New Religious Movement called the Israelites of the New Universal Covenant. I spent every spare moment pursuing that goal and thus put into practice what I had learned in theory, in class, about religious investigative methodology. By the end of 1987, my archive was as full as it was ever going to be. All our Peruvian ministries were again set aside because we were due to travel to Scotland at the end of the year.

Shortly before our fourth furlough I travelled alone to the UK from Peru (29th September–14th October 1987) to be one of the speakers in a RBMU Conference in Swanwick, England. My varied memories include a bone-shaking tropical storm on the flight from Miami to London. I was accompanied by a very courteous couple involved in the Pat Robertson TV Christian ministry in the US. After a rendezvous with the Rev Geoff Larcombe, the RBMU boss in London, I squeezed in a visit to Professor Walls in Aberdeen and caught up with some of my family in Kintore (mother and father, my brother Robert and his wife Setta, and Gordon and Doreen). I left my research archive with my brother in law Gordon and my sister Doreen, in the anticipation of our return to Scotland in 1988. I enjoyed the conference but do remember that rations in Swanwick were sparse! The roast beef had all gone when the plate reached me, and I was only halfway along the table! Aye, and only one roast potato each! Och!

12
Fourth Furlough
1987–1988

> "Don't be impressed with your own wisdom.
> Instead fear the Lord and turn away from evil."
> Proverbs 3:7

It was all go again when we "all four" left Peru for the USA on the 3rd December 1987. Jeannie's mother was by then very ill and just as soon as we arrived, the lion's share of her care fell to Jeannie. It was obviously not the easiest of times to be there. Jeannie's mum (Lena) was holding out for our arrival as she had had a vision or two of Jesus in which she saw his hand brush her own hand. Her interpretation of that dream was that I would pray for her and she would be healed. Jeannie and I asked for a day to contemplate her request. Questions of this nature are always delicate and bring into question how much we ever know of the mind of the Lord. When we did meet for that time of prayer, it was my firm conviction that the Lord was calling her home. I cannot remember how I prayed and though it was not wrong to ask the Lord to heal, I knew on that occasion we had to leave things in his hands. Is it not the age-old tension between leaving and staying with loved ones?

What we both remember is that in mid-January, we were there when Lena's breathing became very laboured and those of the family members who were present met around her bed to pray. On that occasion I do remember praying again and "knew" that it was time to pray for her to enter the eternal presence of the Lord. There was a sense of peace and calm as Lena seemed to relax and quietly breathe her last. It was my privilege to speak at the funeral and to seek to acknowledge that our lives had been enriched by Lena's life. The comfort of Romans 8:35–38 seemed to be an appropriate Scripture to share.

We all arrived in London Heathrow Airport on the 26th January 1988 and Jeannie, still a US citizen, was given entry for precisely one year, under the condition that she register at once with the police! Rebecca and Samuel both held UK passports as well as US ones, and Rebecca also had her Peruvian travel documents. From London we travelled to Edinburgh and to Penicuik, some miles to the West of Scotland's capital city. My Uncle David had found us a two-bedroom accommodation in Penicuik. The Department of Religious Studies in Aberdeen had moved to the University of Edinburgh under its new name: The Centre for the Study of Christianity in the Non-Western World. I was therefore required to complete my PhD in Edinburgh, although because I had previously registered the PhD in Aberdeen, the title was to be awarded in July 1989 by the "auld granite city", from the Faculty of Divinity, and not by the University where I completed my studies.

Rebecca and Samuel, once more, were enrolled in different schools and we were due to live out the year in rather cramped circumstances. Incredibly, we had numerous visitors during 1988 from as far away as Peru. Some relatives in Penicuik (my cousin Kathleen and her husband Michael) helped us accommodate folk when we had no space. The world is small and Mary (nee Sewell) Packer's folk lived close by and we caught up with Alan and Mary as well, and their extended family. Jeannie was soon involved in a ladies' Bible study.

Due to people's kindness, a friend in Glasgow loaned us a car and on three occasions we were given exactly £100 which enabled us to travel three times to Orkney and back, the cheapest ways we could. My days were taken up with trips to New College in the University of Edinburgh and to ten months of intensive writing. What a year! I travelled to Aberdeen to leave the two mandatory copies of my thesis in the university one day before we vacated the house in Penicuik. Once again, we were able to leave debt-free given that I obtained a scholarship to pay my rather substantial full-time fees in my final year of research. We left London two days before Jeannie's visa deadline and we were all back in Lima by the 25th January 1989.

13
Lima
1989–1991

"We do not make our requests of you because we are righteous,
but because of your great mercy.
O Lord, listen! O Lord, forgive! O Lord, hear and act!
For your sake, O my God, do not delay,
because your city and your people bear your name."
Daniel 9:18–19

Unknown to us at the time, we had little more than two years left in RBMU Peru when we returned in January 1989. That kind of knowledge is the Lord's. We found new and comfortable accommodation in a tower block in the district of San Felipe. Before returning to the UK in 1991, we were to move house, yet again, to a house in the district of Lince.

Against the background of being on the move during our time in Peru with RBMU, and with the benefit of hindsight, the stabilising element was that we returned to what we had left in 1987. We attended the same church, Rebecca and Samuel went back to the same school and Jeannie again taught English there. I was involved in teaching/supervising in the Lima Evangelical Seminary and the challenge of the field role of mission co-ordination. I had already written one half of a book[7] in 1987 on the Israelites of the New Universal Covenant, the subject of my still-to-be-written PhD thesis. On return to Peru, the final chapter of my thesis was published in 1989 by the *Revista Teológica Limense,* a Catholic publication, and two chapters of the thesis were published in 1990 in two separate books, this time at my own expense. Stewart McIntosh and Tito Paredes, work colleagues in the Department of Missions in the Evangelical Seminary of Lima, encouraged and facilitated the publications[8]. The books soon sold out although I never saw a penny!

This was all almost incidental to the close fellowship we enjoyed within the ranks of our colleagues. On a personal level, I had two good friends in Ray

---

7 See *Las Sectas. Un Desafío para las Iglesias,* Centro Cristiano de Promoción y Servicios (CEPS), pp 9–48.

8 See *Los Israelitas del Nuevo Pacto Universal — Una Historia* and *Los Israelitas del Nuevo Pacto Universal — Símbolos y Tradiciones,* Ediciones Pusel — Librería "El Inca".

Miller and David Stevens, both very different men in personality and theology, and we worked well together on the field executive. Our family had become members of the Lima Cricket Club so we could use the sports facilities and, more importantly, enjoy fish and chips on a Saturday. As a family we would take time out there. Short-term workers came and went. Indeed, some missionaries came and went.

However, after the arrival of a new pastor, freshly back from studies in Costa Rica, the preaching in our church became somewhat radical. Without revisiting the experience, it seemed to us that every sermon was political in that the "class struggle", "American imperialism" were but a few themes imposed on Scripture. Things had changed drastically, and the final straw came on Mother's Day—an occasion for a great celebration in Peru—when a sketch depicting "Rambo", the American imperialist, killing "poor" Peruvians was central. At a time when poor people were indeed being killed both by insurgents and the military, the whole thing, to put it mildly, was in poor taste. It took me considerable strength of persuasion to restrain Jeannie from walking out. What had become clear to us was that political issues had led the leadership askew and we could not continue. I will allow Jeannie to explain what we did:

> *After a few years in Lima, we changed our church affiliation to the Christian and Missionary Alliance Church [in 1989] where we felt so accepted and welcomed. Our children made friends and frequently spent after school hours at the church, chatting and getting involved in church activities. It was where we were built up in our faith and we were able to see how faithful discipleship could work to establish a thriving church. It was a hard decision to leave Peru and return to the UK when it was time for Rebecca and Sam to finish their education.*

The decision was much bigger than what happened in one particular local church. I was the Mission representative to the Peruvian Evangelical Church in Lima and the pastor of our church just happened to be the chairman of the central board in the denomination in the country. When we announced our change of denominational affiliation, I was duly summoned to the central office and, after what promised to be a heated meeting, some even begged me to reconsider. There was no way back. There are primary biblical doctrinal issues that are not up for grabs, but when secondary teaching takes the place of primary truths, then there is no option. This careful balance led us to a decision that we "knew" we had to take. We remained friends with many of the believers in the local church we left. The Christian and Missionary Alliance Church with its foursquare doctrinal basis—Christ saves, sanctifies, heals and is coming again—and evangelistic/expository preaching, was like music to our ears and hearts.

In the wake of what happened, other missionaries and missions also chose to do the same. Without apportioning blame on either side, Church/Mission relationships at central government level had been strained for years within the

Peruvian Evangelical Church. There are always two sides. What opened up for us, as a family and as a Mission, was a door into new opportunities. We were welcomed into membership and although the large church we joined had a policy of not allowing new members into ministry for six months, after two months I was teaching in their Bible Academy and Night Bible Institute. When I asked them why they had varied their practice in our case, the leaders told me it was because of our "testimony". What they explained was that we had "testified" by our willingness to just attend and be "receptive", "unlike most foreigners"!!

Jeannie, Rebecca, Samuel and I developed lasting friendships in our new church in Lince and we were all sad when it came time to leave our many brothers and sisters in Christ there. The night before leaving Lima, I was invited out by our good friend Pastor Miguel Ángel Gamarra from our new church for a *"cafeciño"* (Brazilian for coffee). Miguel was one of a team of thirteen pastors in the church. During our time together he informed me that, if I had stayed, they would have invited me to join the pastoral team. At that moment I was glad we were leaving. They certainly did not need me, and I knew that I would not have accepted any such invitation. We had witnessed that the Lord was doing a better job through Peruvians than through foreign missionaries. It seemed to me that dependency on western missions had often stunted growth, particularly in the realm of Peruvians developing their God-given gifts. People like me needed to choose a path of taking my place in the shadows.

Change is one of the most difficult things to accept in life. Although we had experienced nothing but change during our married lives, and our children had experienced all the knock-on effects, an even bigger change was looming. Decisions were being made of a new nature in many missions in the world, in part due to the difficult financial viability of supporting so-called small "faith missions". Administrative costs tended to be exorbitant. So it was that RBMU was to disappear into the ashes and rise like a phoenix as part of a new entity. In the Latin case the Evangelical Union of South America and RBMU—what was left of it after India, Irian Jaya, Nepal and Zaire joined other mission agencies—would join and Latin Link was to be formed, with "partnership in mission" as the theme. To cut a long story short, extensive talks went on during the final two years we were in Peru. I travelled to London in May 1990 to be part of high-level talks about this major change. Latin Link has grown since then and has gone from strength to strength and "community with a calling" encapsulates its ideology.

It was with great sadness that we believed that the Lord was leading us home to the UK, and in early 1991 we let our leaders at home and our colleagues in Peru know. We believed it was time to allow our children to complete their education at "home". With a view to a home ministry, I had initiated contact with the Baptist Union of Scotland and all lights seemed green for me to be "fast tracked", as an older more "experienced" candidate (I think), into the Baptist ministry as a pastor. That all changed when Graham Chessman, Principal of the

Belfast Bible College, phoned me to mention that he had heard about me. I discovered later that my name had been mentioned to him by Raymond Pitt (Hamilton Road Baptist Church in Bangor, Northern Ireland) and by some leaders in the Evangelical Union of South America. So it was that we "all four" left Peru on 6th May 1991 for good!

14
Belfast Bible College
1991–1999

"But, my child, let me give you some further advice.
Be careful, for writing books is endless, and much study wears you out."
Ecclesiastes 13:12
"His divine power has given us everything we need for a godly life
through our knowledge of him."
2 Peter 1:3

Our transition into Northern Ireland required some brinkmanship on our part. As mentioned in the previous chapter, we left Peru on the 6th May 1991 and spent some time in the USA. In early June, Samuel accompanied me as we travelled on, via New York, to Glasgow and then to Belfast. The temperature in New York was 90°F on leaving and it was 45°F in Glasgow when we arrived! We stayed with Barry and Anthea Harrison (EUSA reps and lecturers in the Belfast Bible College) while I was formally interviewed by the faculty in BBC.

In my application form I had stated that my postgraduate studies did not qualify me for the vacant position of New Testament lecturer, but that I would happily teach practical subjects, such as Bible books and missions, at College level. New Testament Greek was not my forte. Nevertheless, I had been encouraged to apply. It was therefore with an element of surprise that I received the news that I had been accepted. It was a joy to accept. Terry Paige, a PhD candidate in the University of Sheffield in New Testament, was rightly appointed to fill the official vacancy. The College was growing and by 1991 the student body had risen to its highest ever level of 67 full-time students plus several hundred in part-time courses. In the light of projected growth, they took me on as a full-time lecturer.

Jeannie had become registered as a British citizen in Peru on the 23rd January 1990, so she entered the UK without any problems, along with Rebecca, to catch up with Samuel and me at my sister's in Kintore. After our Orcadian visit, we drove to Belfast in July to take up residence in an empty College, with a view to finding a house in Belfast before classes began in September. A bomb exploded in Belfast on the day we chose to take the ferry from Cairnryan to Larne, so the resulting delay meant that it took rather longer to reach our destination than anticipated.

The next few weeks remain a blur in our memories. Rebecca and Samuel had to be enrolled in Grammar school and we were directed towards Methodist

College Belfast. We looked for a church and were impressed by Pastor Val English in Newtownbreda Baptist Church and by the welcome he extended to us. Val lamented that he was going on holiday for a month and hoped we would continue to attend during his absence. Classes needed to be prepared from scratch as I had eight different subjects to teach, including Reformation Church History at London University B D level. It had always been my least-favourite period of church history to study, and then to teach. After all, I was a Baptist and part of the Radical Reformation. I was also married to an Anabaptist! In record time we purchased, for the first time, a modest mid-terrace in the Erinvale Estate in Finaghy, Belfast and moved in the day before students were due to arrive for their new term of studies!

As a family we were to experience more continuity than ever before. Rebecca was 15 and Sam 12 and they had the opportunity to study in a good school. We made friends and we were active members in our church. Jeannie studied in the Women's Study Fellowship in the College on Mondays from 1992–1995 and then, in 1995, became the Co-ordinator for the programme until we were to leave for Peru again in the year 2000. From January 1992, I was given the added responsibility of being Director of Studies. This opened up for me, not just the opportunity to design timetables, assign subjects to teachers, keep student records, but also to meet all the students to discuss their choice of subjects. Each lecturer also had the added privilege of having a fellowship group, and Jeannie and I enjoyed getting to know so many students. Foreign students were a delight and as the College grew, so did the nationalities within our group. There were times when Spanish was the dominant language when "our" students were in the Scott's house!

I was thrown into a programme so intense that for the next few years I felt, at times, as if it was a question of hand to mouth, like I was driving a car and I knew I was on the road but I did not quite know how I was still on it. Besides lecturing I was often preaching each weekend. When BBC made an agreement to link up with the Queen's University of Belfast, I was able to design my own undergraduate course on New Religious Movements, supervise several MTh students and one excellent PhD thesis. The latter was written on the subject Jesus in the Koran, by the Rev William Long, Church of Ireland Rector in Analong at that time.

During that period of our lives in Northern Ireland, we had many invitations to minister in churches, at conferences and in 1993 and 1994 I was the speaker in Summer youth camps in the Canary Islands run by the Murphy family. Other foreign ministry trips included Poland in the rainy summer of 1997, where we also managed to visit what remained of the concentration camps in Auschwitz. In 1999 we visited our long-time friends, David and Helena Stevens, who were by then working as missionaries in Jaén in Spain with the Spanish Gospel Mission. With the benefit of hindsight, I had still not learned to be selective about invitations.

It was my privilege to work alongside some very fine people in BBC, both lecturers and support staff: Graham Cheesman, James McKeown, Desi Maxwell, Drew Gibson, Lena Morrow, Terry Paige, Isobel Porter, Maureen King, Joan Towell, David Patterson, Susan Clarke… The list goes on. I dare not attempt to list the students who became friends. Indeed, life became busy and yet, Jeannie and I and our two children missed Peru. How does one explain that? For me it was like a bereavement. During my first year I could hardly speak about Peru, even though I lectured on missions. As time went on, I was able to use more illustrations from our time in Peru. Something similar happened when my father died in May 1992. I found it hard, because of the emotions, to give him an adequate tribute at the funeral in Orkney. It took a while to get over his death. Indeed, he still appears in my dreams today, as large as life itself.

What did become clear to me was that Belfast Bible College, with its international and interdenominational student body, was the place for us to be. The ethos was that primary biblical doctrines were fundamental while on secondary issues we could "agree to disagree"[9]. This made sense to me. I had an early introduction to some issues when I was lecturing on the Lord's Prayer in a large Presbyterian Church, somewhere in Northern Ireland, in a programme we called "College On Your Doorstep". After my presentation, two rather larger-than-me, well dressed men stopped me and asked, "What are you?" I remember that I responded by asking, "What do you think I am?" Their reply was: "We think you are a Methodist!" When I asked them how they had so concluded, they explained that I had never once mentioned that "we are elected by God, according to his foreknowledge and in his predestination given eternal security!" Nothing quite like that had ever happened to me before. Nevertheless, I asked if they wanted to know if I believed that, and they assented. Without any difficulty, I firstly clarified that my subject had been prayer but that, "Of course, I believed those truths as they are in the Bible." They stood aside and let me go home!

I suppose that I had never really been bothered about secondary issues, not even as a boy. Indeed, my father's practice of seeking fellowship with any person of like faith was part of my psyche. Study in an interdenominational Bible College, influence from a variety of Christians and churches, eighteen years of mission experience in Peru alongside colleagues from diverse backgrounds, and my own reading from historic writers like John Wesley, John Calvin, Martin Luther and many more-recent Christian writers, had formed me. It is perhaps appropriate at this point to take time and space to affirm that I am an evangelical and that I consider the following cardinal Christian doctrines to be primary: the Trinity, the incarnation of Christ through the virgin birth, the atoning death of Christ,

---

9   Principal Graham Cheesman designed a course—Agreeing to Disagree—for evening class students where we debated "secondary issues". It was a privilege to be asked to chair and to address several such "issues".

the need for repentance from sin and faith in Jesus Christ to be saved, the resurrection of Jesus Christ from the dead, his ascension to heaven, the presence of the Holy Spirit in every authentic believer and the blessed hope that Christ will return one day to complete the Kingdom of God.

John A Mackay went to Peru in 1916 with the Free Church of Scotland and in 1932 wrote *The Other Spanish Christ*. In that seminal writing he argued that the Christ taken to Peru by the *Conquistadores* in the sixteenth century from Spain had been "born in North Africa" and not in Bethlehem. Where the image of that "dead Christ" dominated the understanding of people, the liberating Gospel of Jesus was needed. In Mackay's 1942 book *A Preface to Christian Theology* he illustrated two different ways of understanding theology. There were those who sat on high balconies at the front of Spanish houses watching travellers on the road below. In this way they were theological onlookers without having to regard the practicalities of life. The travellers below, in contrast, faced the problems of life that required, not mere understanding, but called for decision and action. In my journey of faith, I believe I identify more with the travellers.

Mackay writes of personal and "incarnational" mission and that as missionaries, of which I am one, through our service we are given, by the Lord, a platform on which to proclaim our faith. I do not argue with Mackay that the Church of God is made up of the fellowship of those for whom Jesus Christ is Lord. Indeed, he stated that our collective task "is to make Christians". It has long been my belief that sermons, especially missionary sermons, on the Great Commission often emphasise the word "go", but in Matthew's version of the Great Commission, and in other Gospels, that is not the emphasis at all. Only one verb in Mt. 28:18–20 occurs in the imperative mood, and that is the verb translated "to make disciples". Perhaps it would be better to translate the verse, "Therefore, going, make disciples…" What is important is that Jesus commands his disciples to make disciples. The going is almost taken for granted and refers to wherever we find ourselves in the world as we follow Christ.

A person becomes a disciple when he or she identifies him/herself with the community of those who believe in the Father, Son, and Holy Spirit. This is done through baptism. A person grows as a disciple when he or she is taught everything Jesus commanded. Nowhere does Jesus mention a person being evangelised, becoming a Christian, being converted, or joining a church or denomination. Jesus does not command his disciples to do any of those things. Rather, he tells them to make disciples, a longer, but more complete process. And so, it has continued down to our time: disciples are to make disciples. This is to continue until "the very end of the age". That would sound like a daunting proposition without Jesus' encouraging words, "I am with you always". The one who possesses all authority in heaven and on earth promises to always be with His disciples as they carry out His mission to make disciples. What might sound unachievable is now seen to be certain.

So, I have written down in print what I believed by the time I started to teach in the Belfast Bible College and what I believe today. I am a "traveller" and have chosen not to sit on the balcony. The colours of my theology are those of black and blue and, like every disciple, I continue to travel. Life was busy and Jeannie and I found ourselves working seven days a week. Jeannie was mother, wife, WSF Co-ordinator and she had also taken on some child minding to enable students and their wives the time they needed to study and work. The College itself had grown since 1991 with its student body of 67 full-time students to 150 in 1998[10].

In that milieu, Jeannie and I were praying about our own future and were considering either ministry in Scotland or a return to Abancay in Peru. I had already visited Latin America (Costa Rica, Peru) in 1993 in order to do some research for the Centre for the Study of New Religious Movements in Selly Oak Colleges in Birmingham. In early 1997, I travelled to Peru and to Bolivia to visit personnel in a Mission agency and to visit Apurímac. After much prayer, we decided not to return to Abancay (27th February 1998) and some days later (1st March 1998) we decided to politely decline the invitation to take up a pastorate in Scotland. At that time, and out of the blue, Claude and Aileen Macquigg, members of the church we attended, suggested that we give prayerful consideration to joining Charlie Anderson and John Brew (Baptist Missions — Peru) who were starting a Seminary in Moquegua, Peru in 1998. So we prayed and asked to meet Pastor Derek Baxter, Director of Baptist Missions.

Later that year, as part of my sabbatical, I was due to travel to Peru to teach in the Evangelical Seminary in Lima. As part of an exchange, Dr Samuel Escobar was to travel to Belfast and teach in the Belfast Bible College. I think Northern Ireland got the better deal. Everything was happening quickly. Someone on the Board at BBC gave money so that Jeannie could travel later in 1998 and catch up with me in Lima after I had finished teaching. With regards to "spying out the land" in Moquegua, we were open to that possibility, so prayed for the £200 we would need to pay for our fares from Lima to South Peru and back to Lima. That prayer must have gone directly to the Lord before we prayed and back to the donor. We received a £200 cheque in the mail from someone on the 4th March 1998 specifically to make our journey to South Peru. So it was that we were able to travel to Peru in July 1998, fulfil our commitments there, apply to BM, be accepted, and by the end of 1999 prepare for yet another challenge to "travel" some more.

---

10 See Kenneth Scott, 1998, *Sited for Service. A Short History of the Belfast Bible College.*

15
Baptist Missions
2000–2007

> "So don't worry about these things, saying,
> 'What will we eat? What will we drink? What will we wear?'
> These things dominate the thoughts of unbelievers,
> but your heavenly Father already knows all your needs.
> Seek the Kingdom of God above all else, and live righteously,
> and he will give you everything you need.
> So don't worry about tomorrow,
> for tomorrow will bring its own worries.
> Today's trouble is enough for today."
> Matthew 6:31–34

Several things happened along our route into Baptist Missions. At the end of 1998, as part of my application for Baptist Missions, the required medical examination revealed that I was in danger of developing diabetes type 2 due to "reduced glucose tolerance". It was timely to be given that diagnosis and life changes were made regarding diet and exercise. Here is a conundrum for the medical profession where countless doctors who gave me advice attributed diabetes type 2 solely to lifestyle. In my family, only two (Tom and Martin) of us seven brothers have not developed type 2 diabetes. The Christian doctor who diagnosed me also advised a reduction in stress. So I learned that too many cakes, too much weight and too much stress combine to raise sugar levels. The Peruvian diet included fresh fruit and vegetables and that helped during our time with Baptist Missions. Ah, I confess that a very helpful diabetic nurse advised me about finding a substitute that tasted good and that did not contain sugar! I have blessed the Lord many times for her and acknowledge that from that time I developed my taste for good coffee!! I have included these details because I was also becoming aware of the aging process.

More importantly, we were faced with a new test of faith. I well remember when an elder from our church came to us with a letter the church leadership had received from Pastor Derek Baxter. The nameless elder—he knows who he is—was incredulous that our annual allowance in Baptist Missions was to be about £4,600, plus expenses. Amusement spilled over into more disbelief when I assured him that the letter was accurate and that there was not a missing two or one before the four. Nevertheless, Jeannie and I had to be sure that the Lord was leading because our outgoing expenses at home (mortgage, house insurance and rates) were about £300/month. Rebecca and Samuel continued to live in our house and covered the utilities. So Jeannie and I did draw in a breath but can testify that we were sure that the Lord was leading us. Therefore, our trust in the Lord would not be in vain. We are happy to include the comment years later that we never used our field allowance to pay for home expenses. Such details illustrate what a man of faith had once told me: "Along the way the Lord always places integrity tests in our way, and we do not move on until we pass them." In this regard Jeannie and I had long-since learned to make it a practice never to ask for money for ourselves, but only for projects.

Our Commissioning Service in Newtownbreda Baptist Church in the year 2000 was a once-in-a-lifetime experience. Stanley Graham, the NBC church secretary at the time, ably chaired the evening. James McKeown, Vice Principal of the Belfast Baptist College, brought greetings from the College in his eloquent manner. Staff and students accompanied Dr McKeown that evening. Derek Baxter outlined what God was doing in Baptist Missions. Pastor Francis Gordon from the Kirkwall Baptist Church was present, thanks to someone in our church who paid his airfares. He had been a good friend to Jeannie and me over the years and it was nothing less than special to have him there. His words kept me grounded in the midst of praise too high for me to recognise myself. We remember that the church was packed, and the service culminated in the laying on of hands and prayer from the elders. Before Desi Maxwell, one of my very good friends[11], preached and challenged us to live life in the Spirit, he sang a song[12] that he had originally written a year earlier. Of the nine verses, five will suffice here:

> Our bonny wee lad is called Kenny,
> The wee lad was born on Orkney
> Today as we gather he's fifty
> Oh bring back those years gone so swiftly…
> OH HE'S FIFTY, HE'S FIFTY, OUR KEN IS FIFTY TODAY, TODAY
> BUT HE'S NIFTY, AND THRIFTY, OUR KEN IS FIFTY TODAY
> Our bonny wee lad has some body
> He works at it every day
> His muscles they can pump iron
> But now there are signs of decay…

---

11 Desi Maxwell, James McKeown and I were nicknamed the "three musketeers" in Belfast Bible College.

12 To the tune of: "My bonny lies over the ocean". Written by Desi Maxwell on the 3rd February 1999 to celebrate my 50th birthday on 30th January 1999. Desi had originally sung it at our staff farewell in Belfast Bible College.

> Our Kenny is famed for his braces
> And in tartans oft he is found
> But now he needs both belt and braces
> For gone is that tummy so round.
> Our Kenny is known as a Baptist
> Of water he is fond we all know
> But all the Presbies just love him
> Though their level of water is low.
> Our Ken is well loved by the students
> To them he's quite a sage
> But now they will hold him in reverence
> Because he has reached old age…

It is a healthy balance here to include what Jeannie writes about our move to Tacna:

> *Exactly twenty-five years after my first arrival in Peru, we returned once again to work in Tacna in the very south of the country. We were going to work with a different mission, among people from a different culture from the ones we had lived with, in a situation that had all the comforts of home. All our past experiences and life-skills were put to use. Ken set up a Seminary in Tacna and as part of it I set up a study programme for women. It has been a particular joy to me to know that that programme has continued to provide women opportunities to study and develop ministry skills. I taught some English classes in the Seminary and worked with women's groups in a couple of local churches. I helped establish the library in the Seminary, coding the books and placing them on the shelves where they should be.*
>
> *Life was easier than at any other time in Peru, but I had left our children at home and that was very difficult for me. I was really a wife and mother. That was my calling, and I was bereft without Rebecca and Samuel. Any ministry I did outside the home I considered incidental or extra. Both our children were working and no longer in their teens, but we had always been "the four of us" and I felt the separation terribly. Computers were on the go and we could "dial up" and chat with them if we didn't get cut off! The Mission graciously allowed us to return home to Northern Ireland every year for two months, and that made the separation more tolerable.*
>
> *God is faithful, he is sovereign and uses all our experiences, both good and not-so-good, to teach us and prepare us for the next step in life. In Psalm 38:8 the Lord says: "I will guide you along the best pathway for your life. I will advise you and watch over you."*

Before we arrived in Tacna, Peru in 2000, Irish Baptists had been active in seeking to plant churches in Peru since 1924[13] in what was then known as the "Irish Baptist Foreign Mission". Indeed, both in Puno and in Tacna, different missionaries had set up Bible Institutes over the years. None of those activities should be forgotten and the lack of mention here is simply because, in more recent years leading up to our arrival, missionaries were involved in more diverse ministries. Their story has been told and will be outlined in Baptist Missions' publications in the future. By the time of our arrival in Tacna, several "veteran missionaries", such as Desi and Mavis Creelman and Andrew and Rachel Lovell, and other support missionaries, had returned home after years of service. For some reason I was often mistaken for Desi Creelman. Of course, he is a handsome fellow!

A new thrust into training Peruvians for ministry came when Charlie Anderson and John Brew had begun classes in 1998 in Moquegua in the Mitchell Memorial building. The term that would normally have begun in April 2000 was postponed so that they could reorganise some of what they were doing in Moquegua. This came as a blessing to me as I took my time to visit pastors, churches and to get work done on the "Baptist Centre"[14], a three-storey building in the southern part of Tacna. Pastor Derek Baxter had given his blessing on those activities and also, after discovering some anomalies in documentation on buildings, in BM employing our first full-time Peruvian administrator. Money was raised, Alicia Quispe was employed and a lawyer friend of Alex Campbell, Reynaldo Macchiavello, was paid a retainer fee to help with all things legal.

We began classes in Tacna in September 2000 with over sixty evening class students. At that time, and following the pattern in Moquegua, there were full-time students for whom Charlie Anderson, John Brew and Trevor Morrow had raised scholarships. I also raised money for students, one of whom was Elizabeth Almanza. She was known to other missionary families for her maturity in the faith and started full-time studies in September 2000 in Tacna. Once she had completed her studies, she became the administrator of the Seminary in Tacna. She was an indispensable member of the team from the beginning and continues today. I would travel through to Moquegua along with John Brew during the week to teach there and drive back the same night. We both also taught in Tacna. It had been agreed that Jeannie and I should take two months back in Northern Ireland each year both to be with our family and to promote the expanding teaching ministry in Tacna during our furlough

---

13 See Andrew Reid, 2000, *By Divine Coincidence. A History of the Irish Baptist Foreign Mission 1924-1977*, Published by The Association of Baptist Churches in Ireland, for an excellent account of and reflections on the early period of missionary activity by Irish Baptists in Peru.

14 This was a two-storey purchased by BM. Alex Campbell had added a third floor.

meetings. We used the time to raise funds for the subsequent year. To be honest it was good to be paid a basic pastor's salary for two months each year at home. In our previous mission, our field allowance continued on home leave.

While on our first furlough, Pastor Baxter arranged for us to meet a couple who then donated a single gift of £30,000 ($40,000 at the time) for an additional building to be erected in the patio of the Baptist Centre in Tacna. Indeed, this led me to the beginning of a new role that was to continue during all our time in Tacna, somewhat akin to that of a project manager. It was amazing that the gift received was sufficient to pay for the three-storey multipurpose building and all its furnishings. Alex Campbell had taught me the ropes by example as he had already overseen the construction of three large church buildings in Tacna.

However, on the 23rd June in 2001 at 3.33pm, South Peru was struck by an earthquake[15] that measured 6.8 on the Richter scale in Tacna and lasted for one minute and 40 seconds. Considerable damage was done to the Baptist Centre, although the new building, still under construction, remained intact. In the aftermath, time was devoted to giving aid to many affected by the earthquake and to extensive repairs to the original structure. Pastor Baxter arrived soon after the event and officially opened the still-incomplete building. Derek came with Pastor Alan Baird and a team of folk from home. Alan was President of the Association of Baptist Churches in Ireland, for the first time during 2001–2002, and we were to develop a good friendship in years to come.

The new building served us well and there were over 100 students regularly enrolled in Tacna in part-time, full-time and postgraduate studies. The students represented a diversity of church affiliations in the city. Jeannie rose to the challenge of setting up the Women's Study Ministry and it has always been an important element within the Seminary in Tacna.

2002 was a year of consolidation and we had begun to cast our eye, along with Derek Baxter, over two plots of land facing the Baptist Centre which comprised of a two-storey building adjacent to a larger vacant lot. I had spoken to the owners several times, but they did not want to sell the property as they were projecting building a school there. On return to Tacna in early 2003, Jeannie and I were joking one day as we drove home from lunch in the centre of Tacna and Jeannie (jokingly) suggested we should "name it and claim it"[16] as we drove over the vacant lot. I remember that I replied: "Why not?" We entered our flat and asked the Lord to change the owner's mind. Not ten minutes had passed when, in response to the doorbell in the patio below, the owner of the property asked me directly: "Señor Scott, would you like to buy the property?" I had only one question: "How much?" We took it as an answer to prayer and Pastor

---

15 See Appendix A for an account of the experience.

16 Not vocabulary that we used because of the inherent dangers attached to such presumptuous language when taught by "silly" people.

Baxter was immediately on the case and the $40,000 was in our hands within two weeks.

By the end of 2003, another multipurpose building, including classrooms, offices and an auditorium, was almost completed. The offering of the May Mission meeting of the Baptist Association in Northern Ireland was designated to pay for the chairs to be installed. Pastors Derek Baxter and Gordon Darragh (Missions Director in-waiting from November 2003) were there for the formal opening of the new buildings in early 2004. Before the end of 2003 I was, I have to confess, struggling with the idea of pulling out of the Seminary and of starting a Christian Radio Station in Tacna. I was still battling by this stage in ministry, to focus on one major thing at a time. With a radio ministry in view, my priority was to find a suitable site on which to build a custom-made building. Such a property became available for us to purchase on the other side of the same block diagonally opposite the auditorium we had just completed. Milton Paz Berríos, the Christian architect I had befriended, was again called upon to draw up the plans for the radio building before our next short furlough at the end of 2003.

Overhead projectors were tools used on furlough at that time and I remember using a projected image of the building we planned to build in 2004. It was one thing to plan to erect a state-of-the-art building and quite another matter to obtain a radio license and to design the programmes. I had never done anything like this before and as I had consulted several people who knew much more than I did, they suggested that I visit a large radio ministry called HCJB (Heralding Christ Jesus Blessings) in Quito, Ecuador. With that in mind, I began to think of how much it would cost for me and my good friend Reynaldo Macchiavello (our Mission lawyer) to travel there and back. I remember that I told Jeannie, and no one else, that I was asking the Lord for £1,000 ($1,800 at the time) to make the journey. It was after I preached in my home church and that I had mentioned my desire to start the new ministry and my plan to visit HCJB (without any mention of money) that a member approached me afterwards and specified that the Lord had laid on his heart to offer me £1,000, precisely for the journey to Quito. He asked whether it would be enough! My reply was: "It is an exact answer to an exact prayer!"

A few months after returning to Tacna in 2004, Reynaldo and I travelled to Quito, Ecuador from the 16–18th July. We both learned much as we met folk there from HCJB and we sought to imbibe all the advice available. It was the right thing to do at that time and we were promised a satellite dish, to be delivered to Tacna as and when we could use it. This would enable us in due course to download their programmes. Legal Statutes were drawn up and the "Sower Radio" (*Radio Sembrador*) was officially born on paper. It was later in 2004 that I started a one-hour service on Monday evenings during term time in the Seminary. "The Bible Hour" began in September, designed to include congregational worship, a Bible reading, prayer and exposition of Scripture. The sixty-minute recordings were designed to be radio programmes. Seminary classes were adjusted so that students could attend, and invitations were extended to churches announcing the innovation. As attendance grew the new auditorium was where we developed our first locally-produced programme.

In the meantime, and as money was raised back in Northern Ireland, I returned to the task of being a project manager. This involved me in a search for a current radio license in Tacna but the government ministry for radio diffusion, centred in Lima, had already granted Tacna its quota of licences. A start was made on the building with its sound-proofed walls designed for use as a radio station. I made numerous trips to Lima in search for equipment and suitable personnel. At this point it is better to shorten the history of what became a more drawn out process than anticipated. The building was completed in 2005, the satellite dish was delivered safely from Ecuador and we began to transmit programmes on the Internet from 2006 onwards. This meant that we were already working full-time. With help from Reynaldo, we managed to buy another radio station, the only way to acquire an existing license, and then to install the requisite mast on a hill above Tacna and, more importantly, legally transfer the license into the Sower Radio. It was with great joy that the Sower Radio FM 105.1 was finally able to transmit on a 24-hour basis from April 2007. By that stage Rubén Mendoza and his family had been head-hunted in Lima as the Radio Technician, while locally-selected Raúl Sánchez and Daisy Lozano were the presenters and Blanca Valenzuela the administrator.

Although I am tempted to include more detail, I wish to go back in time to the year 2003, to recount that, while in Northern Ireland, I enrolled in a new Master of Arts in Theology degree (from the University of Wales, Lampeter) offered by the Irish Baptist College. It was a pleasure to study the courses and to write the dissertation. I was to complete my degree and graduate *en absentia* in 2005 and then managed to matriculate Elizabeth Almanza, Jorge Aguirre and Silas Ramos[17], three of our Seminary personnel, in a new academic year in 2005. Jeannie travelled to Northern Ireland with them on the 24th August 2005 and stayed on after their intensive studies, with Elizabeth Almanza, to return on the 23rd September.

I will never forget having received a phone call from Jeannie in late August when she tearfully told me that our son, Samuel, had been diagnosed with cancer. This was and is any parent's worst nightmare. Jeannie was the BM treasurer in Peru, so she quickly did what she had to do in disbursing funds and Lourdes Williamson (Graham and Lourdes Williamson joined BM at the end of 2005) took over her role. Jeannie left Peru again on the 2nd October to look after Samuel.

That was a difficult time. I recall sitting down with Jeannie before she left for home and we divided up our field allowance between us—we were paid on a

---

17 All three eventually completed the degree after a "little" (a lot!) of help with their written English!

three monthly basis—she took two thirds and I remained with one third. On arrival in Northern Ireland, Gordon Darragh kindly loaned Jeannie a mission vehicle and both Gordon (recently treated for cancer) and Samuel (with cancer) changed a flat tyre together. Not many weeks into Jeannie's time at home, she phoned me on Sunday morning, just as I was about to go to church, and said, "Ken, I have no money!" My reply was: "Neither do I so all we can do is pray!" Does the Lord not hear our prayers before they even get to heaven? After all, it is He who guides us to pray. The next day Jeannie received a £500 cheque from somewhere in Scotland, out of the blue, from a person who felt constrained to send it. It was a comfort and Jeannie eked it out to cover expenses as Samuel was also penniless. I travelled home on the 11th December 2005 and was glad to be with Samuel during his last chemotherapy treatment. Much prayer was raised for Samuel, and although he was declared to be in "remission" before we returned to Peru on the 7th February 2006, we left Northern Ireland reluctantly.

It has been good to reflect with hindsight and now at this distance and after this lapse of time. Jeannie and I thank the Lord for our eight years in BM Peru. During 2006 we managed to purchase another property adjacent to the auditorium complex—BM now owns half of that block of buildings—and I was glad to be occupied again as "project manager"! Jeannie started a bookshop in that building in 2007 along with Meche de Ocaña. Jeannie and books are always a good mix. I had handed on the oversight of the Seminary before that time with over 100 students and with the ability to offer accredited degrees. I particularly enjoyed the camaraderie and fellowship with the Sower Radio team and sharing good coffee with them. That too was handed on, to Lourdes Williamson's oversight and to the team, along with the "Bible Hour".

Jeannie and I knew by 2007 that it was time to leave. Our work was done. Although there was more to do, it was not to be done by us. We knew that the team out there was more than capable of doing a better job than us. It was time to retire from what we had started. Perhaps, in part, we had had the wind knocked out of our sails through Samuel's ordeal and we simply knew that we needed to be with our family. Gordon Darragh had been a good friend to us, and we had shared our thoughts with him. It was a surprise to me when Billy Colville (ABCI Director), Hamilton Moore (IBC Principal) and Edwin Ewart (IBC Principal-in-waiting) asked to meet me while in Northern Ireland in early 2007, and even more so when they proposed that I might join the Irish Baptist College Faculty after leaving Peru later in the year.

16
Irish Baptist College
2008–2014

> "Keep on asking, and you will receive what you ask for.
> Keep on seeking, and you will find.
> Keep on knocking, and the door will be opened to you.
> For everyone who asks, receives.
> Everyone who seeks, finds.
> And to everyone who knocks, the door will be opened."
> Matthew 7:7–8

During our time in Tacna, Jeannie and I had enjoyed visits from our home church from Roy (NBC Mission Committee) and Elaine Lyttle, Stanley and Irene Patterson, the late Marion Moreland, John (NBC Mission Committee) and Helen Robinson and, indeed the Robinsons' son, Stephen. Ex-students from BBC and family members from Scotland and the USA had also ventured out to see us. The NBC Mission Committee had extended support and prayer on our behalf and, on our furloughs, we were glad to be given time and care by the McLaughlins, Raymond and Helen Davis, John and Helen Robinson, and others. Pastor Derek Baxter, BM Director, amazed us during his tenure by meeting us at the airport in Belfast each time and by making a vehicle available to us on furloughs. Likewise, Pastor Gordon Darragh, his successor, facilitated a mission vehicle and, more importantly, long chats.

We returned to a changing home church scene when we landed in Northern Ireland in October 2007. Pastor Freddie and Linda McLaughlin had been installed in Newtownbreda Baptist Church soon after we left for Peru in the year 2000. Up until then, the church had sustained itself numerically during a three-year pastoral vacancy and had implemented an ambitious building programme. Subsequently, we had become aware, on each succeeding yearly furlough, of rapid church growth that resulted in the addition of over 100 new members during our time in Peru. For that we rejoiced. On the other hand, while we were mistaken more than once for being new to the church, we also did not know many of the new folk. What had represented subtle small changes for those attending each week had struck us as something more radical each year, especially when we remembered how it was when we had left eight years before. Jeannie and I had to sort out in our minds and hearts which of the changes were good or whether we were fighting against changes that needed to come.

It was Gordon Darragh, and the BM Peru Committee, who had asked me to consider taking on a role of co-ordinating BM's "Reach into Belfast" programme on a half-time basis. This would have given me full employment as the role in IBC as director of the postgraduate programme would have been the other part-time ministry. After careful reflection I decided that I should not accept BM's offer. Fine Northern Irish missionaries were involved in the Reach into Belfast programme and I knew that as an "outsider" it would not have been appropriate for my involvement. I made the same decision later when it came to linking up with Newtownbreda Baptist Church and the Haypark Avenue outreach. To be honest I knew what it was to work at the cutting edge of mission in Peru and to have witnessed "jostling" for ministry. I am slow to recognise evidence of jealousy or envy in ministry but with the passage of time I believed that, when evident, it required me to stand aside. I also knew that, even although I had worked in a teaching ministry in Northern Ireland, I still did not presume to understand the nuances of cultural divides in the Province.

That decision meant that from January 2008 until January 2010 I was not fully employed, and I will always be grateful that in the providence of God I had time and space to settle in. I occupied my time by preparing classes, cooking, preaching regularly and I also enrolled privately in a distance-study programme with the University of Wales, Lampeter. I thoroughly enjoyed studying for a Licence in Theology (equivalent to a Graduate Diploma) that acted as a refresher course in The Book of Genesis, Patristic Theology—The Making of Orthodoxy, Religion in the Contemporary World and culminated in a research project entitled *An examination of the presence of Andean Messianic Expectations in three Peruvian New Religious Movements*. I developed the latter into a book in Spanish, published in 2016. With regards to preaching, I accepted numerous invitations and also preached during the vacancies of more than one Baptist church. I had long-since learned to clarify that I would not consider any pastorate. I was/am a missionary.

Jeannie had been supportive in all the above developments and she sought employment and was successfully accepted as a full-time sales assistant from the 1st November 2007 in the Faith Mission bookshop in Lisburn. This was the Lord's provision in helping us to pay the bills. Jeannie was in her element in recommending and finding books for customers, although she admits to some challenges when it came to developments in technology. Both our children, Rebecca and Samuel, got married in the year 2010 and Anjali Sophia Pillai was born to Ganesh and Rebecca on the 20th December 2012. Samuel and Claire's marriage ended in divorce. Jeannie left her employment in August 2013 to help Rebecca look after Anjali. Becoming grandparents opened up for Jeannie and me a new world that was full of joy, and yet again, when Ajay Scott Pillai was born on the 7th September 2017.

Gordon Darragh had come back to me and persuaded me to take up a role as BM Promoter. So from 2010 until retirement in January 2014, I spent four years in full-time employment. It was a privilege to work under Gordon as BM

Director and alongside the Faculty in IBC (Edwin Ewart, Alan Baird, the late Maurice Dowling, Peter Firth, David Luke, Nigel Younge and Valerie Hamilton). They were all kind to an old man who had a lot of catching up to do in a world of new technology. It had always been a joy to teach students and to witness their walk of faith with the Lord and into ministry.

During two years (2008–2009) Alan Baird and I shared an office in IBC and we became good friends. He was to accompany me on eight of my subsequent twenty return visits to Peru. Jeannie went with me only once. It was my privilege to be accompanied by a team of pastors on one occasion, by Mervyn Scott twice, Brian Davison once—an elder from my home church—and to allow them (and Alan) to do almost all of the teaching. I was more than content to accompany them, to translate and take my place as the organiser. It was in God's providential leading that Jeannie and I ended our "official" working lives as we did. Nevertheless, Peru was still not out of my system at that time.

17
Retirement
2014–

"But the godly will flourish like palm trees…
Even in old age they will still produce fruit;
they will remain vital and green.
They will declare, 'The Lord is just! He is my rock!
There is no evil in him!' "
Psalm 92:14.
"Remember your leaders who taught you the word of God.
Think of all the good that has come from their lives,
and follow the example of their faith."
Hebrews 13:7

When I was young, I was guilty at times of thinking that older people had always been that way. Perspectives came into the equation: in my teens, those in their twenties were getting on in life. Later, in my mid-twenties, forty was certainly not far from old age. When in my mid-forties, I well remember a godly man from the Crescent Church in Belfast, now in glory, saying, "Ken, fifty is downhill, sixty is faster, and seventy, all the way!" One sure thing is that seventy has come fast and for the last few years Jeannie and I have been saying to each other on our birthdays: "How have we arrived here?" Now, as I sit among the old folk, I consider eighty to be old! I apologise!

The first major change that came with retirement in January 2014 was that I gave up my two part-time jobs. I was no longer the Postgraduate Studies Director in the Irish Baptist College or Mission Promoter in Baptist Missions. That meant I received no more wages from the Association of Baptist Churches in Ireland. I continued to lecture in the College, preach by invitation and travel to Peru. The Mission Team in Newtownbreda Baptist Church, instead of continuing sending support for me to Baptist Missions, recognised my ongoing role as an associate missionary of BM and agreed to pay my basic expenses on Peru visits. Since January 2016, I have been directly responsible to my home church and the Mission Team have paid my expenses to and from Peru. Without this I would not have been able to continue visiting the country I had come to love.

Furthermore, I was still preaching. I did notice that the frequency of preaching opportunities dropped from 30 times in 2013, to 15 occasions in 2014, to 6 in 2015, to 5 in 2016 and again another 5 in 2017. It was in 2017 that I began to pray about whether I was becoming "yesterday's man" as far as preaching was concerned. By 2018 I had decided to dedicate myself to writing. For many years I had continued to avidly read and collect books on Peruvian history, religion and culture and had also continued to research, more-at-a-distance, the Peruvian Israelites of the New Universal Covenant. Although the research had been on the back burner, as it were, I completed a book in Spanish at the end of 2015 that was published in 2016[18]. It outlines both a history of some Peruvian Andean New Religious Movements over the centuries and also my preferred methodology of research. I completed another book in Spanish in October 2018 that, at the time of writing this, was to be presented in Lima, Peru in April 2019. I was "relieved" when I turned down eight preaching invitations in 2018 and also when I chose not to accept the invitation to teach in the Irish Baptist College. I started this book in November 2018 and have been scouring my files since then as I sought to include important life events.

I am getting ahead of myself. Several people encouraged me to continue to teach in IBC and others said that there is nothing in the Bible about retirement! Actually, all good intentions aside, there are reasons why some of us should step out of certain ministries. Age is not just a number. A cursory reading of Ecclesiastes chapter 12:1–7 makes that clear. Furthermore, everyone is different and my decisions have not been reached lightly. Having passed the nadir of middle age, I have never been more content in life than now. An ideal day for me is to get up reasonably early, drink a leisurely cup of tea—we do crave a cuppa as we get older—read my Bible, and take my time to pray and meditate.

Incidentally, my methodology of Bible study, developed over the years, is not complicated. For those who have written books on "how to" and for us who have taught the same, I confess that what I do now does not follow the books or lectures. I have learned to vary my approach by either reading entire chapters, to gain an overall perspective, or I study a particular passage in more detail, including a few verses within their context, and dig into them a little. I suppose that the main questions I bring to my reading are to ask the Lord to teach me more about Himself, more about how to live as a Christian and what the Scriptures might mean for me in my own life here and now. The particular tasks and pressures that lie ahead that day are part of any time of prayer. Meditation emanates from thinking everything through in the presence of God, both then and during the day, while prayer is talking to God about it all. Nothing substitutes for personal devotions, and personal application of Scripture is quite separate from any preparation for teaching or preaching. The latter two ministries require more digging and build on a personal walk with God.

Only after devotions comes my first cup of filter coffee, now a half-caff due to doctors' orders, and a breakfast roll. One of my pre-retirement wishes was to be

---

18 Kenneth D. Scott Eunson, 2016, *Nuevos Movimientos Religiosos Andinos. Un acercamiento interdisciplinario,* Ediciones Puma.

able to walk to a bread shop each day and buy fresh low-GI rolls, followed by fresh filter coffee. That is what I do and, besides, I try to walk between 3–5 miles daily. Jeannie and I make it a practice of praying together after breakfast. I am never happier than when I am "interrupted" by my grandson, Ajay, on any given day, so that I can be with him, either travelling on the bus into Belfast or on an extended walk to the park. Childhood passes so quickly, and he and I have often bonded together and placed the ills in the world in their proper perspective. Life is good.

I thought I would include some indications of aging, just because I want to. What about the following list? We feel stiffer, talk a lot about our joints/ailments, groan when we bend down, do not know any songs in the top ten, misplace glasses/bag/car keys/etc., get more hairy (ears, eyebrows, nose, face, etc.), we avoid lifting heavy things due to back concerns, we say "in my day", we find it tricky to sit cross-legged on the floor, we hate noisy places (church?), we choose clothes and shoes for comfort rather than style, we fall asleep in front of the TV most evenings, we think policemen/teachers/doctors look really young, we fall ill more often, we say "it wasn't like that when I was young", we complain about more things, we need an afternoon nap, we feel tired the moment we wake up, we struggle to use technology, we find we have no idea what "young people" are talking about, we have colleagues who are so young they don't know what a cassette tape is, we lose touch with everyday technology such as tablets and TVs, we complain about the rubbish on television these days, we spend time comparing illnesses and injuries with friends, our friends are all ill more often, we do not know or remember the name of any modern bands, we consider going on a "no children" holiday, we never go out without our coat, we put everyday items in the wrong place, we move from Radio 1 to Radio 2 (actually, I listen to Classic FM), we start driving slowly, we struggle to lose weight easily, we buy a smart phone but have no idea how to do anything other than make phone calls on it (my granddaughter Anjali, who is six years old, teaches me), we feel we have the right to tell people exactly what we are thinking, even if it isn't polite (well, my mother did!), we pay by cash or by cheque rather than using our card, we are told off for politically incorrect opinions and, to cap it all, our ears are getting bigger! I rest my case!

I need to get back to writing seriously here. Jeannie and I spent our lives placing our faith in the Lord and in His providential leading. Despite all the twists and turns of life, we came to not depend on money, security and prestige for life, but in all that God promised to be for us in Christ. The Scottish scholar James Denney once stated that "it is impossible at the same time to leave the impression both that I am a great preacher and that Jesus Christ is a great Saviour. In the same way it is impossible at the same time to give the impression that I am a great Christian and that Jesus Christ is a great Master". In the light of a truth like that, we are all challenged to seek to live for the glory of God.

If you, the reader, have followed these accounts of my life stories to this point, you will know that I believe in the worldwide task of disciple-making (Matt.

24:14; 28: 19–20; Mark 13:10; Luke 24:47–48). Jesus Christ is to be proclaimed as God incarnate, Lord and Saviour; and God's invitation to find life through turning to Christ in repentance and faith is to be delivered to all. I also believe that all Christians, and therefore every congregation of the Church on earth, are called to practice deeds of mercy and compassion, an all-encompassing neighbour-love to all forms of human needs as they present themselves (Luke 10:25–27; Romans 12:20–21; Matt. 9:36; 15:32; 20:34; Mark:1:41; Luke 7:13).

In contrast to that, John Stott wrote in 1978, "A chorus of human voices is chanting in unison that at all costs I must love myself". Stott's challenge was that spiritual maturity did not lead to being assured of no storms in life, but of being people, in Christ, that no storm could destroy. It does seem, at times, that the priority is to have high self-esteem, to be healed of all our damaged emotions and to express the need to feel fulfilled. Those are no substitutes for being able to rest comfortably in the Lord who gives no guarantees about storms in life or indeed, of blessings. Just as we find in Scripture that Job did not know the reasons behind his sufferings, we are not guaranteed good health, nice families or a good final salary. I suppose we confuse this so-called goal of finding self with that of finding Christ.

Society around us has also been changing rapidly in the West. The gap between wealth and poverty has become more extreme. With the widespread use of developing technology there is a growing tendency to over-sensualise and to be more preoccupied with human physical appearance. Luxury goods and an obsession with food represent good viewing on television and on the media. Xenophobia and fear of outsiders has led to isolationism[19]. John Stott coined the phrase that the Gospel needed to be "counter-cultural". Indeed, after living in a country where we witnessed poverty every day, it took Jeannie and me time to come to terms with a more wealth-oriented worldview. Furthermore, like all Christians, we struggle not to simply imbibe many of the values that surround us each day.

Love in Action became a charity that took shape in my heart in 2015. I had been asking the Lord increasingly for a way of demonstrating the "compassion" of Christ, that inward aspect of the neighbour-love that led Jesus to heal the sick, feed the hungry, and teach the ignorant. I was challenged when Alison Boyd, sometime previously, had presented Newtownbreda Baptist Church's plan for a food bank called Sustain. I knew that I wanted to help destitute children in Tacna, Peru and had already experienced something of the credibility that this could bring to any Christian's profession of faith. Christ makes us sinners into those who love God and all our fellow human beings.

---

19 I owe it to conversations I have had with my son Samuel to being able to articulate several of the changes that have happened all around us in society in the West during the last few years.

After speaking to two elders in my church (John Robinson and Raymond Davis) and then being given the OK by the elders and Mission Team in Newtownbreda Baptist Church, Ágape en Acción (Love in Action) was legally begun in Peru in early 2016. It took a little time, and several visits to Peru by me, to get it up and running. Nevertheless, for three years, numerous destitute church-connected children were helped in Tacna, Peru. They were mainly given donations of food and this, in turn, benefitted the entire family. There were many needy cases. The help was made possible through support given from a select and modest number of people, known to me, and to them. I have always found joy in working behind the scenes. Did not Jesus counsel us to seek Him in secret and not to do our good deeds "before men"?

I considered each one of the Peruvian Love in Action team in Tacna to be a friend and all were members of different evangelical churches in Tacna. For your information, they were Reynaldo, Wilmer, Epifania, Bertha, and Mabel. Luz María López Carpio (single Christian mother of Valentina — born on the 2nd April in 2014) was employed 20 hours/week from Love in Action funds. Luz coordinated the administration of Love in Action from the beginning and was crucial to its development. Several people went the extra mile and gave generously in 2017 (£4,000) for Luz's mother, Yaleny, to have an operation on a life-threatening aneurysm in her head. Yaleny's life was certainly saved, although she is now blind in her right eye.

The plan was never for me to continue indefinitely in Love in Action. Indeed, from its inception, there was always the understanding that I would hand over by my seventieth birthday in January 2019. As we prayed about the future of Love in Action, Jeannie suggested to me that we hand on our office equipment to Rubén (ex-director of the Sower Radio) and to his wife, Rosa. In the subsequent interchange between Luz, Rubén and Rosa, Luz gave them a copy of the Love in Action constitution. Rubén and Rosa, unknown to us, asked the Lord that we would offer them the charity. It was while praying one morning that I wondered whether we should not offer them Love in Action. When I mentioned this to Luz, she informed me that she also had come to the same conclusion. The others agreed and Rubén and Rosa were overjoyed.

I have been humbled by how the Love in Action charity developed, and has now been handed on to others. During my visit to Tacna in November 2018, the new committee was installed. The new members have taken over everything including the office, the bank account and the legal entity. I could not be more satisfied by the outcome. It was what I promised leaders in Newtownbreda Baptist Church in the beginning and it is what the Lord, in his wisdom, has led us to do. For me, to start Love in Action and then to leave it in good hands, has been an exciting experience of faith behind the scenes and one of the greatest joys of my life.

I acknowledge that the glory is the Lord's. My gratitude extends to those who gave faithfully and to those who prayed. I could not have played my part without the support of many, my home church and John Robinson's wise counsel along the way. Partnership with Peruvian brothers and sisters in Christ has been a joy. This adventure of faith will stop for me but will continue for those in Tacna.

18
Reflections

> "One can give without loving
> but one cannot love without giving."
> Amy Carmichael

As a Christian, Christ calls me to live my life as His disciple. His own example and teaching in the Gospels made it clear. I know more clearly now than ever that I am called to go through this world as a pilgrim, as a mere temporary resident, travelling light. I am still learning to be willing, as Christ directs, to give up material wealth and the security it provides and to live in a way that involves me in relative poverty and the loss of possessions. My treasure is in heaven and I do not need to be too concerned about budgeting for treasure on earth, nor for a high standard of living. I may be required to forgo both because I am called to follow Christ, carrying my cross.

Dietrich Bonhoeffer, a German theologian struggling to follow Christ in the midst of Nazi rule, penned one of the great Christian books of the twentieth century. In it he wrote that the first call every Christian experiences is "the call to abandon the attachments of this world". The theme of the book is summarised in one potent sentence: "When Christ calls a man, he bids him come and die." Bonhoeffer aptly entitled the book *The Cost of Discipleship*.

Jesus said the same as Bonhoeffer long before him. In Luke 14, Jesus laid out the cost of discipleship: "If you want to be my disciple, you must hate everyone else by comparison (v.26)... And if you do not carry your own cross and follow me, you cannot be my disciple (v.27)... So you cannot be my disciple without giving up everything you own (v.33)".

When and if God denies me something, it is only in order to make room for one or another of the things He has in mind. Sometimes, I still presume that a person's life consists (partly, at any rate) in the things they possess! How true is this statement by Saint Augustine. "Earthly riches are full of poverty".

In the light of the challenging call to follow Christ, I certainly evaluate myself as a fallen creature, not strong and self-sufficient as I may have at times supposed, but weak, foolish and indeed bad. Unless the grace of God had intervened, I would have headed for hell and not for glory. I have come full circle and acknowledge that I continue to give all I know of me to all I know of Christ. This personal relationship relies always on Christ giving Himself to me. Indeed, I still ask for His mercy and rest on Christ's undertaking to make me clean for Jesus' sake.

The venerable Bishop Ryle is reputed to have said: "Heaven is a prepared place for a prepared people, and they that enter shall find they are neither unknown nor unexpected". It was as if Jesus said: "We have no lasting home here on earth, but my Father's home is a home where we will be together for all eternity". Heaven is a home which is permanent. Jeannie and I are entering our final phase before glory itself.

All of my life has been one of living "by faith" and there are incredible life experiences that have happened by the grace of God. Jeannie said "yes" when I popped the question and she has been a rock throughout my life. Rebecca was born, Samuel was born, I earned a PhD, I taught in the Belfast Bible College (8 plus years, September 1991–December 1999) and in the Irish Baptist College (half-time January 2008–January 2014), Jeannie and I served over 26 years in Peru as missionaries (January 1973–September 1991 in Latin Link, and January 2000–December 2007 in Baptist Missions), I served as an associate missionary with Baptist Missions from January 2010 until January 2014 and in retirement Love in Action gave me so much joy. Since leaving Peru at the end of 2007 "for good" I have returned twenty times. I conclude this paragraph briefly by stating that the call of discipleship on my life will always place Christ above all else, then my lovely family (Jeannie, Rebecca and Ganesh, Samuel, and, of course Jeannie's and my two beautiful grandchildren, Anjali and Ajay). Although I thank God for all that Jeannie and I may have "done", I know that over and above everything, Christ's call is "to be" like Him. This leads me inevitably to my final biblical reflection.

Agape

In 1 Corinthians 12:31 the Apostle Paul wrote to the believers in the church in Corinth and gave them advice about their narcissistic use of the gifts of the Holy Spirit (chapters 12 and 14) in the following words: "But now let me show you a way of life that is best of all" (NLT version).

The book by Clive Staples Lewis (1898–1963) *The Four Loves*, published firstly in 1960, and the biblical text quoted above, together serve as the basis for my final reflections. Lewis wrote about four words translated from the Greek New Testament as "love" in English. The four words are *agape* (Christian love or God's love), *storge* (the feeling of affection for someone), *eros* (the feeling of desire for or the need of someone or to feel attraction, especially in either sexual or estetic contexts) and *filia* or *philia* (the attitude of friendship and/or to reciprocate the friendship).

Agape refers to the unique love of God now present in the Christian according to Paul: "For we know how dearly God loves us, because He has given us the Holy Spirit to fill our hearts with His love" (Romans 5:5). Each one of the other three words, "natural loves", represents a mixture of animal instinct, of personal likes, of consciousness and appreciation, and of the impulse to please oneself, so that in this way each word is radically different from *agape*. "The natural loves" declares Lewis (2016: pg 141)[20] "are not auto-sufficient". So when Paul wrote his letter to the Corinthian Christians, it was to challenge them with his words. "But now let me show you a way of life that is best of all". The challenge is to live out *agape,* the content of which is spelled out in 1 Corinthians chapter 13. This is the standard of living which continues for all of us who call ourselves Christians and disciples of Jesus Christ.

C.S. Lewis (2016: pg 37) wrote in 1960 about a book he himself would never write but that needed to be written. He was referring to the need for a complete confession from those who represent Christendom regarding the specific contribution of Christianity to the sum of cruelty and human betrayal. He declared that many sectors of the world would not listen to our message until we could publicly reject much of our past. This is the challenge to practise *agape*. *Agape* is "a way" of action and affirms four related truths:

1. This pathway of life means that we do good to others and, in some way, exalt them. *Agape* is an expression of gratitude towards God for His treatment of us in Christ. We make God great as we exalt Him in worship, in thanksgiving and in obedience. In a similar fashion as we "love our neighbour" we express this in exalting them and as we meet their observed needs. So, *agape* is demonstrated in each and in every human relationship.
2. *Agape* cannot be measured by sweet words, nor by strength of feeling, but by actions and, even more specifically, by the self-sacrifice expended in order to accomplish this purpose.
3. *Agape* takes the initiative to help where there is need and finds joy in helping for the benefit of others. *Agape* automatically does something good where there is need, even when the recipient does not deserve the help or good and does not restrict itself to help those who deserve help.
4. *Agape* focuses on specific people with specific needs and prays and labours to free the person from wickedness. In every occasion and event *agape* takes hold of God and of His love in Christ as the supreme example, as it is revealed to us in the Gospel. We confess that without the work of God's grace in us we are not able to live this "better way" of *agape*.

As I enter what is the final phase of life, before the joy of meeting my Lord and God, my prayer for me and for all who know Christ, is that we might give due attention to "being" like Him rather than give priority to "doing" for Him. God will be the final judge of the extent to which we have walked the "better way" of agape. It is a joy, without equal, to wake up and live each day in the anticipation of our heavenly Father's welcome of yet another "unworthy servant" into heaven.

---

20   C.S. Lewis, [1960] 2016, *The Four Loves*, William Collins: London.

"The Lord bless you and keep you;
the Lord make His face shine upon you;
The Lord lift up His countenance upon you,
and give you peace."

Appendix A
When the Earth Trembles

This is a transcription of my article, first published in the Association of Baptist Churches in Ireland's magazine Irish Baptist Life, *September 2001, page 15. John Brew and Charlie Anderson also wrote their perspectives about the earthquake in the same edition of the magazine on pages 16 and 17 respectively.*

On Saturday the 23rd of June 2001 at 3.33pm, John and Lourdes Brew and we (the Scotts) had lunched together in a restaurant and had returned to the Baptist Centre where we were relaxing and drinking coffee, when an earthquake of 6.8 on the Richter scale struck. On the way out of the building, in close pursuit of Jeannie and the Brews, I remember thinking two thoughts. One was the concern for the workmen who were on the scaffolding on the outside of the new building three floors up. They managed to scramble in through the windows. The other revolved around the possibility of the Lord taking away the yet uncompleted extension and its anticipated potential use.

We experienced a very long one minute and forty seconds as the road came towards us like waves of the sea, the two Baptist Missions' vehicles danced with the earth, and the Baptist Centre swayed and developed cracks before our eyes. When it was over, the question was what to do about the last week of classes, and the official inauguration of the new building and graduation planned for Friday the 29th of June. I decided it should be business as usual.

During the final week of classes, several students (and who could blame them?) stayed away. In the meantime, Pastor Derek Baxter[21] had arrived with a team from the Emerald Isle, but without their baggage. He managed to be present (between trips to the airport) for his part in the official opening of the new building, dressed in one of John Brew's suits matched with his own white trainers!

The two-hour programme seemed short and we rejoiced as we sang the Baptist Centre's theme song. "We are the people of God' and its chorus…And we will take His glory to each nation and town, taking them hope and news of salvation, and His love motivates, as we are not able to keep quiet; we will announce His love and truth to the world."

---

21 Pastor Baxter was the Director of Baptist Missions at the time and he had arrived in Peru, along with a team, very soon after the earthquake.

Pastor Alan Baird[22] challenged us to make knowing Jesus and His Word the goals of our lives. Special music came from Peruvian singing groups like Ebenezer, from Jeannie's English classes, and from the Irish team. John Brew gave our first certificate to Javier Astete and our diploma to Pastor Timoteo Álvarez. They will both continue to study towards higher qualifications. People did not rush home afterwards but made short work of the refreshments.

The earthquake had changed many lives and we know the Lord uses catastrophes of life for purposes beyond our understanding. He has the right to change our plans and to bring them into line with His own. Since then, the same classroom was transformed into a storeroom for products from two agencies in order to help the victims of the quake in Tacna. Several students were involved in its distribution and it has been a joy to reflect on the past few weeks and see how the Lord has brought His people together from the many churches in Tacna. By God's grace, the Baptist Centre's still uncompleted extension has been pivotal in that scene.

God's presence was frequently marked by earthquakes in Scripture and Habakkuk 3:6 states "He stood and shook the earth…" and comments on other calamities by concluding "yet I will rejoice in God my Saviour. The sovereign Lord is my strength… He enables me to go on the heights."

Our task for the future is to seek the direction of His Spirit and to follow Him as closely as possible.

---

22 Pastor Baird was President of the Association of Baptist Churches in Ireland, for his first term of service (2001-2002), at the time. He was President for his second term (2018-2019) and now for a third term (2019-2020). Alan and I became good friends and have travelled to Peru together eight times over later years.

Appendix B
Health and Wealth

This appeared as my article in the May 2003 edition of the Association of Baptist Churches in Ireland's Irish Baptist Life, *pages 16–17; reprinted in* Insight, *August–September 2019, pages 12–14.*

The visiting evangelist from Lima communicated well as he preached in a Baptist church in Tacna. There was a rapport with the congregation as they constantly answered his questioning "amen?" with their affirmative "amen". He carefully preached blessing as the outpouring of material goods on those who would but give more, believe more and put God's spiritual laws into practice. Finland was chosen as an example of a country that followed these laws and, consequently, of being the wealthiest nation in the world! The preacher presented his own past sinful life and subsequent faith in Christ as another example of the Lord's blessing and of resulting personal wealth.

We were twenty minutes into an appeal before I decided to leave. On exiting the church, I saw one man's scowling face, as he muttered, "It is easy to see why he is preaching and whose pocket he wishes to fill." Others did not seem to share that conviction as they moved to the front with offerings and with hearts set on seeking God's "blessing".

I have been surprised at two things in regard to the "health and wealth" teaching as witnessed in Peru. Firstly, it is frightening to see what is actually taught. Secondly, I am shocked by the gullibility of church members as they accept it and its implications for their lives. Having stated that, I wish to approach the subject, not as one who has any monopoly of wisdom, but as one who constantly needs to humble himself before the Lord and recognise the need for the illumination of the Holy Spirit in order to discern truth and error as outlined in the Bible.

Those who propose a "health and wealth" theology argue that God loves us so much that He has a marvellous plan for the physical and financial blessing for each of His children. Their ideas owe much to western optimism and affluence, especially since the Second World War. There is no doubt that those who follow this thinking believe they are preaching a "pure" gospel. For them material prosperity represents a means by which faith and spirituality may be measured by the application of recognised laws of prosperity, such as sowing and reaping. It is also perceived that if a Christian is not rich, he or she is simply demonstrating a lack of faith, is not practising the laws of prosperity or has some hidden sin. Little emphasis is placed on the time-tested wisdom that prosperity results from work, a simple lifestyle, savings and investment. Instead there is "naming and claiming it", which consists of positively affirming something so that by visualisation it becomes a reality.

We have become used to reading books and to hearing testimonies and sermons, where the authority of what is claimed is supported only by statements like "I feel", "the Lord revealed to me", "the Spirit showed me" or some similar expression of feelings. But surely our main concern should revolve around the centrality of the Word of God, which exists not to reaffirm our prejudices or presuppositions, but to correct them. We need to be close to the apostolic faith which we say we have inherited.

Kenneth Copeland (*The Laws of Prosperity*, 1978, Tulsa: Harrison House) presents the logic behind what developed into the "health and wealth" theology. He claims that powerful laws exist which control the physical world, and even God Himself is subject to what He created. It is a believer's faith that makes these laws function. In the final analysis the implication is that we may manipulate the sacred in our favour, which in this case means health and material prosperity. We are therefore redeemed from poverty, sickness and even death! This is far from the Gospel of Jesus Christ which states that we are redeemed from our sin, the world and the Devil.

Of course, no one wishes for a church of poor people, nor is it wise to ignore the fact that God may wish to prosper Christians of His choosing. That is not the issue here. What is at stake is the manipulation of Scripture in order to focus our attention on a message promising health and wealth in this life through following certain spiritual laws. In spite of an abundance of "testimonies" cited in order to back up the "soundness" of the health and wealth teaching, we need to return to Scripture and allow it to speak.

It is dangerous, however, to study any topic as an isolated biblical theme. It is too easy to appeal to Scripture in order to claim authenticity for a particular stance. The health and wealth we discover in Scripture comes from the original creative purpose of God. Salvation is something that touches our whole being as we believe in Jesus. Physical wellness and wealth are only two aspects of greater blessings in the Lord.

The Scriptures warn us about certain dangers of wealth:

> Keep falsehood and lies far from me; give me neither poverty nor riches but give me only my daily bread. Otherwise, I may have too much and disown and say, "Who is the Lord?" or I may become poor and steal, and so dishonour the name of my God. (Proverbs 30:8–9)
>
> For the love of money is a root of all kinds of evil. Some people, eager for money, have wandered from the faith and pierced themselves with many griefs. (1 Timothy 6:1)

In the next section I would like to contrast the "health and wealth" ideology to that of Scripture. This should enable us to be more discerning and to seek to follow the Lord more closely.

Health and wealth	Biblical theology
The goal is human wellbeing.	The goal is the glory of God.
It is based on the power of faith (positive thinking) which rests in believing in the power of language.	It is based on the power of God, on the merits of Jesus Christ and on the sanctifying work of the Holy Spirit.
Sin is the lack of power or of technique.	Sin is separation from God.
Salvation represents success, wellbeing and power.	Salvation is reconciliation with God.
The Bible is a manual for success.	The Bible is the Word of God.
Revelation is in dreams or in particular "information" from God.	Revelation is all the Word of God.
The successful Christian life is power, wellbeing, a comfortable lifestyle, and to have "one's own universe".	The successful Christian life is to be a servant of God, to seek holiness and to be made into the "image of Jesus".
Holiness—is to have victory.	Holiness—is humility before God.

Group study

I realise the message of "health and wealth" is sometimes presented more benignly than in the picture I have painted. Its teaching does challenge us to be discerning and to examine our own biblical belief systems in order to evaluate whether we are preaching the true Gospel. May I suggest that you, the reader, use this redacted article, and the biblical texts below, as the basis for reflection. Some biblical texts used as a basis for the "health and wealth" teaching:

> Proverbs 6:2; Matt. 7:7; Matt. 11:24; Matt. 21:22–23; John 10:10; John 16:23–24; Romans 4:17; 3 John 2.

Some biblical replies to the "health and wealth" teaching:

> 2 Chronicles 1:11; Psalm 62:10; Proverbs 13:2; Matt. 6:33; Matt. 10:8; Matt. 20:25; Matt. 23:12, 26; Galatians 5:22–23; 1 Timothy 6:9–10; 1 Peter 5:5.

One of the worst nights of my life is worth a mention here. This story was not included in the above article as it had not happened still. Further, it represents an extreme view of health and demonology. It happened like this. About a year after the above experience, and my subsequent reflection, I received a phone call from Pastor Pedro Santos, an Assemblies of God pastor in a large church in Tacna. His church was to have a visit from two Korean preachers and, unfortunately, the interpreter had fallen ill. Pedro asked me if I could translate for them. I discovered that the two Koreans in question had been in Peru for two years and they preached in English through a Peruvian interpreter. I had two questions. I needed to know that the Koreans spoke good English and the core of the message I was going to have to translate. To the best of his knowledge, Pastor Santos assured me they had good English and that they would only preach the Gospel.

So it was that I turned up to a packed church and met the two Koreans. First impressions were that they were both immaculately dressed, although I had also donned my suit and tie and had polished my shoes. Alarm bells began to ring when, as I was introduced to them by Pastor Santos, it was almost impossible to communicate with them in either English or Spanish. I had not been told that the interpreter normally had a manuscript in English, and he had been with them for two years. I was not offered any written text. Indeed, it became clear that one of the two would preach and the other appeared to be even less adept at either language. I was praying that I would do a good job of translating and in my heart dismissed my doubts about the task by thinking that they were maybe just preoccupied before speaking.

It was after the preliminaries and the time of enthusiastic worship, cut short in order to give maximum time to the preaching, that I began to have my worst fears confirmed. From the first word I had difficulty in understanding the preacher's English. Nevertheless, I was there to translate. So it was, little by little, that I faithfully sought to repeat, word for word, the "Gospel" message being preached. I was hearing myself repeat the sermon: "if you are sick, you have a demon, and if you have a demon, you can be delivered tonight." Indeed, the preacher assured them that plastic bags had been brought and that after the message they would be able to vomit the demons into a bag. In the blur that followed, besides going from hot to cold, I remember that attempts were made at quoting verses to justify the message. Everything in me was crying out against what was happening. I was tempted to leave but stuck to my unenviable task. I remember the preacher giving an example of his own wife having been sick and once she had vomited up the demon, she was well. "Hallelujahs" rang out from some present at this "testimony", and at the preacher's pleas of "amen?" I also remember, at one stage, being unable to understand completely the word "Atán" in English. To his annoyance I stopped and asked him to repeat the word more than once. Finally, I understood he was referring to Satan. It was with relief, after what seemed to be an eternity, that we reached the end of the sermon, but the beginning of the appeal. I was still there and witnessed those coming forward. The other Korean then moved among several people, who were mostly contorting, offering them plastic bags. I had had enough and when the preacher on the platform went into a long pause, I left the building. On my way home in the first taxi I could hail I determined to call Pastor Santos the next day.

In all fairness Pastor Santos called me first. He apologised and informed me that the Assemblies of God, the biggest denomination in Tacna and in Peru, decided that those men, with that message, were not preaching the Gospel and that they should be banned from Assemblies of God churches. I was relieved. I should add that all Koreans do not preach like them. As for myself, I considered what I did to be a mistake. Several months later I was teaching a course for my good friend Dr Tito Paredes in Lima in the *Facultad Evangélica Orlando Costas* and mentioned the experience. One of his lady teachers had been present that evening and told me about the fallout.

A German by nationality, she explained that some had watched my face change from white to red and all kinds of colours. I am sure that was true and demonstrated the inward turmoil I went through. Anyway, some suggested that I was the one changing the content of message to such extremism while others recognised that I did not want to be there. Unfortunately, others were only too happy to accept the message as given. I choose to include the story. My regret is that I became the mouthpiece of what is not finally the Gospel.

I want to briefly add an account of one more similar experience in Tacna. It was in my second year in Tacna that I learned of a Pentecostal pastor who had died of cancer. His death had been prolonged and painful, and he had left a widow and several small children. A group of students in the Seminary approached me to ask if I was going to his church because two "prophetesses" had predicted he would be raised from the dead. When I answered in the negative, they wanted to know if I had no faith to believe in that miracle. I remember answering, I believe graciously, that I had the conviction that the Lord had taken him home to heaven. I could include graphic tales of what I was told later, but simply want to conclude by stating that while his widow and children were left devastated by a further disappointment, the two "prophetesses" left Tacna quietly.

Appendix C
Humility is a Pilgrimage

Originally published in ABC Insight, *February–March, 2016, pages 14–15.*

Preamble

I remember someone telling me of the author of an autobiographical book who stated that his life "had always been characterised by that humility which is the mark of all truly great men." My Christian upbringing, Celtic blood and my late father's words; "I can't stand a braggart", "never brag" accumulate to make any claim of that nature repulsive.

I am reminded of a little poem I heard many years ago.

>Once in a saintly passion I cried in desperate grief
>"Oh Lord my heart is dark with sin as I am chief."
>Then stooped my guardian angel and whispered from behind
>"Vanity my little man you are nothing of the kind."

This is only a poem but illustrates the other extreme. False humility. Indeed, I wonder if more Christians tend towards the inferiority complex end of things rather than to any superiority complex. It is reprehensible to demonstrate human superiority over anyone but is equally so to envisage another with any sense of envy[23]. Both poles are undoubtedly motivated by pride. Where do we find a balance in life when we are encouraged, for example, in job interviews, to "sell" ourselves and our qualities? Some advertised opportunities for full-time employment in Christian ministry invite the same approach. Surely our Christian lives should not be defined so much by the status gained through our professional qualifications and the ensuing salaries as by our response to the biblical call to discipleship.

Humility and Discipleship

Dietrich Bonhoeffer, a German theologian who struggled to follow Christ in the midst of Nazi rule, wrote one of the great Christian books of the twentieth century. In it he wrote that the first call every Christian should respond to is "the call to abandon the attachments of this world". The theme of his book is summarised in one powerful sentence: "When Christ calls a man, he bids him come and die." He aptly entitled his book *The Cost of Discipleship.*

---

[23] Galatians 5:26: "Let us not become conceited, or provoke one another, or be jealous of one another".

I remember visiting a Christian and Missionary Alliance Church in Lima in 1974, days after arrival in Peru as a new missionary[24]. What I witnessed changed my life. The local church was experiencing phenomenal growth and blessings. It was self-governing, self-propagating and self-supporting, with a discipleship programme I have seldom seen duplicated. The experience led to a steep learning curve. Any thoughts of self-importance or self-interest[25] as a missionary were overtaken by the glory of God in action and the need to be humble[26] like those Peruvian Christians.

Playing Second Fiddle

Leonard Bernstein said in response to a question of what was the most difficult instrument in the orchestra to play: "The second fiddle. I can get plenty of first violinists, but to find someone who can play the second fiddle with enthusiasm, that's a problem. And if we have no second fiddle, we have no harmony." John the Baptist played "second fiddle" to Jesus. John 3:30 records his declaration regarding Christ: "He must increase, and I must decrease."

Growing in Grace

The Apostle Paul grew in humility as he aged. Around AD 56, Paul wrote: "**For I am the least of the apostles,** who am not even worthy to be called an apostle, because I persecuted the church of God." (1 Corinthians 15:9). Around AD 61, he wrote: "**To me, who am less than the least of all the saints,** this grace was given, that I should preach among the Gentiles the unsearchable riches of Christ." (Ephesians 3:8). Around AD 64, shortly before his death, Paul wrote: "This is a faithful saying and worthy of all acceptance, that Christ Jesus came into the world to save sinners, **of whom I am chief."** (1 Timothy 1:15). The Scriptures leave us in no doubt as to what God thinks of our pride and our need for the humility that leads to "more grace"[27].

An Application

We are all just as humble as the choices we make in regard to our discipleship of Christ. We follow Christ because He chose to be born for us, to live as a slave for

---

24 With a mission that is now called Latin Link.

25 Philippians 2:3: "Let nothing be done through self-ambition or conceit, but in the lowliness of mind let each esteem others better than himself."

26 Philippians 2:5: "Let this mind be in you which was also in Christ Jesus."

27 James 4:6-7: "But he gives us more grace. That is why the Scripture says: 'God opposes the proud but gives grace to the humble`. Submit (humble) yourselves, then, to God. Resist the Devil, and he will flee from you." James 4:10: "Humble yourselves before the Lord, and he will lift you up."

us, to die as a sinner on the cross for us, to be raised from the dead and to be exalted for us (Philippians 2:6–11). Indeed, the greatest reason for Christ having humbled Himself was to rescue a lost world from the second death. Christ's values were the opposite of this world's where self-importance and self-interest reigned. The New Testament encourages us to edify, receive, welcome, greet, look after, submit to, forgive, confess our failings to, share hospitality with, to esteem others as better than ourselves and to love (fourteen times) each other. The challenge to choose to be humble, is daily and continuous.

"He must increase, and I must decrease."

Appendix D
Thoughts on Leadership

Published as "Still learning—personal thoughts on leadership", in Insight *(Association of Baptist Churches in Ireland), October–November, 2018, page 26.*

There can be little doubt that humble, unassuming people make the best leaders. This does not mean that narcissistic leaders (I too had to look that one up) may not have a devoted following. There are people who like them!

The Scriptures call for humility[28] and when Jesus draws a lesson from His teaching on the Shrewd Manager (Luke 16:8)[29] is He not emphasising the need for sanctified common sense and for the priority of developing good interpersonal relationships in leadership?[30]

The following are a few lessons I am still learning along the way, from the examples of others and often, to my shame, from painful experience:

- A good leader does not brag about being one!
- Restraint in emitting judgements is paramount
- The competent leader helps give guidance to others
- Patience includes passion and the ability to pause and reflect
- Availability requires commitment and time for people
- Remaining impartial may require the leader to temper his/her own views
- Setting the agenda and developing the team requires prayer and planning
- A leader will not ask another to do what he/she would not do him/herself
- Rudeness and/or bullying, sows conflict and confusion
- Involvement in committees requires preparation for them to be taken seriously
- A leader should demonstrate ownership in all prep work
- A leader is a facilitator and representative of others in the group

---

28 For example: "No, O people, the Lord has told you what is good, and this is what he requires of you: to do what is right, to love mercy, and to walk humbly with your God." (Micah 6:6). "As the Scriptures say, 'God opposes the proud but gives grace to the humble.'" (James 4:6).

29 "And it is true that the children of this world around them are more shrewd in dealing with the world around them than are the children of light."

30 Luke 16:9 "Here's the lesson: Use your worldly resources to benefit others and make friends."

- Leaders make mistakes and need to admit them
- Sensitivity to the nuances of perceived good leadership can vary from one culture to another
- Unfortunately, some folk cannot be led, and some people should not lead
- Indeed, those who cannot follow should not lead

Due to human complexity there is no magic formula. Nevertheless, humble leadership contributes most to a collaborative environment. A biblical leader exalts the Lord and at the same time exalts others. The quickest way to take away from the centrality of Christ's overall leadership, is when the leader seeks to present him/herself as great. It does not work. Instead we are to "esteem others as better than ourselves." I have had the privilege of being led well and I trust I have treated others in the same way. Ask them! Sooner or later most of us will be challenged to hand over our leadership. There is never a greater challenge to our taking the path of humility. The grace of God always precedes and follows such a choice.

90231744 M